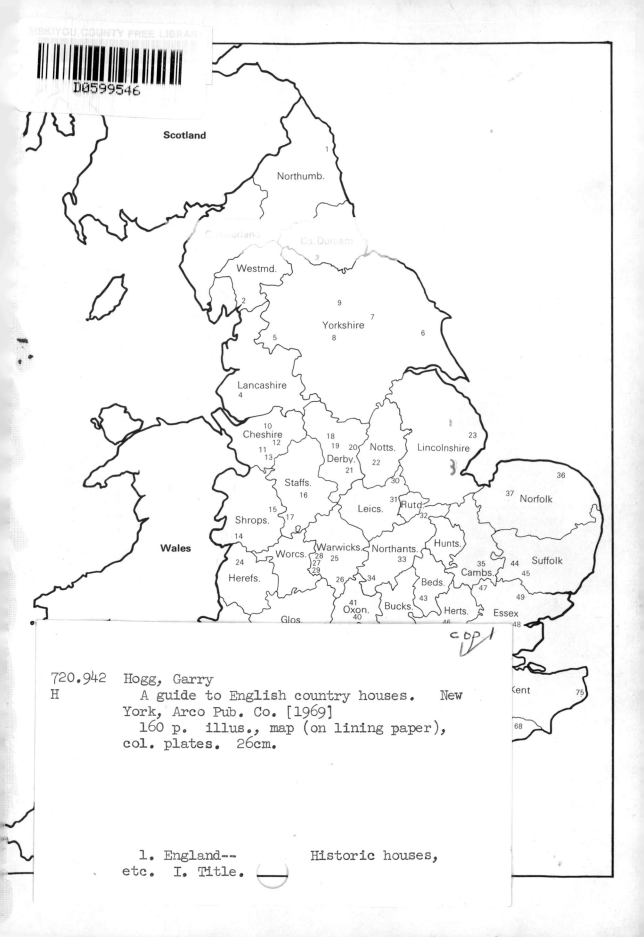

720.942
H

Hogg, Garry
    A guide to English country houses.   New
York, Arco Pub. Co. [1969]
    160 p. illus., map (on lining paper),
col. plates. 26cm.

1. England-- Historic houses,
etc. I. Title.

A guide to English Country Houses

A guide to English Country Houses

Garry Hogg

Arco Publishing Company, Inc.

New York

Acknowledgments

Aerofilms and Aeropictorial *front of jacket*, 84 ; Barnaby's Picture Library 34, *56;* British Travel Association 14, jacket flap and 22, 26, 32, 40, 60, 62, 64, 66, 68, 70, 76, 78, 80, 86, 88, 94, 98, 100, 102, *110,* 114, 116, 120, 122, 124, 132, 138, 140, 142, back of jacket and 144, 146, 150, 156, 158 ; J. Allan Cash 118 ; Central Press Photos 44 ; Country Life 24, 42, 48, 58, 82, 96, 104, 106, 132 ; Eagle Photos © Bill Bawden 12, 30, 50 ; Albert W. Kerr 46 ; A. F. Kersting ½ *title,* 10, *20,* 28, 112, *126, 128,* 130, 136, 152, 154 ; Keystone Press Agency *36, 54, 74,* National Monuments Record 16 ; Oriel Press *frontispiece, 92;* Ormskirk Advertiser *72;* M. Percy *108;* Picturepoint *18, 38, 90,* 148 ; Reece Winstone 52.

half-title page Beaulieu Abbey
frontispiece Capesthorne

Published by Arco Publishing Company, Inc. 219 Park Avenue South, New York, N.Y. 10003

Library of Congress Catalog Number 70-90891
Standard Book Number 668-02080-6

Printed in England by
Cox and Wyman Limited, Fakenham

Contents

Foreword 7

Bedfordshire   Woburn Abbey 10

Buckinghamshire   West Wycombe Park 12

Cambridgeshire   Sawston Hall 14

Cheshire   Adlington Hall 16
Capesthorne 18
Gawsworth Hall 20
Little Moreton Hall 22

Cornwall   Cothele House 24

Derbyshire   Chatsworth 26
Haddon Hall 28
Hardwick Hall 30
Melbourne Hall 32

Devon   Chambercombe Manor 34
Powderham Castle 36

Dorset   Athelhampton 38
Forde Abbey 40

Durham   Raby Castle 42

Essex   Audley End House 44
Beeleigh Abbey 46
Hedingham Castle 48

Gloucestershire   Berkeley Castle 50
Dodington House 52

Hampshire   Beaulieu Abbey 54
Breamore House 56

Herefordshire   Croft Castle 58

Hertfordshire   Hatfield House 60

Kent   Chartwell Manor 62
Hever Castle 64
Mereworth Castle 66
Penshurst Place 68
Walmer Castle 70

Lancashire   Rufford Old Hall 72

Leicestershire   Belvoir Castle 74
Stapleford Park 76

Lincolnshire   Gunby Hall 78

Norfolk   Blickling Hall 80
Oxburgh Hall 82

Northamptonshire   Burghley House 84
Castle Ashby 86
Sulgrave Manor 88

5

Northumberland	Alnwick Castle 90
Nottinghamshire	Newstead Abbey 92
Oxfordshire	Blenheim Palace 94
	Rousham House 96
Shropshire	Stokesay Castle 98
	Weston Park 100
Somerset	Cothay Manor 102
	Montacute House 104
Staffordshire	Blithfield Hall 106
	Wightwick Manor 108
Suffolk	Ickworth 110
	Melford Hall 112
Surrey	Clandon Park 114
	Polesden Lacey 116
Sussex	Arundel Castle 118
	Bateman's 120
	Glynde Place 122
	Great Dixter 124
	Parham 126
	Petworth House 128
Warwickshire	Charlecote Park 130
	Compton Wynyates 132
	Coughton Court 134
	Packwood House 136
	Ragley Hall 138
Westmorland	Levens Hall 140
Wiltshire	Avebury Manor 142
	Longleat House 144
	Lydiard Mansion 146
	Wilton House 148
Yorkshire	Browsholme Hall 150
	Burton Agnes Hall 152
	Castle Howard 154
	Harewood House 156
	Newby Hall 158

The houses are listed alphabetically in the index at the end of the volume

Foreword

The official publication, *Historic Houses, Castles and Gardens in Great Britain and Ireland*, lists some four hundred of these in England alone. From among them I have had the invidious task of selecting seventy-five great houses. In making my selection I was guided by two main principles : first, to distribute the great houses as widely as possible ; second, to give some indication of the whole range of them by including not only the largest and best known 'stately homes' but also the smallest, those less often visited, but equally worth seeing. It is frequently the case that a house of modest pretensions, very much off the beaten track, and little advertised, proves to be a gem that amply repays the time, effort and perseverance put into locating it.

So I have included in this volume great houses to be found in thirty-three of our forty-odd counties (excluding London and Middlesex). They range from Alnwick Castle in Northumberland to Beaulieu Abbey on the South Coast ; from Walmer Castle in Kent to Cothele House in Cornwall ; from Blickling and Melford Halls in East Anglia to Croft and Stokesay Castles almost on the Welsh Border. As for the second principle, they range from such vast mansions as Woburn Abbey, Blenheim Palace and Castle Howard, at one end of the scale, to little jewels such as Beeleigh Abbey and Levens Hall. For some visitors it is the magnificent that appeals, the heroic in scale ; for others it may be the more intimate charms of the smaller house, the cherished home.

In a book such as this there is not the scope to do more than offer a hint or two as to what awaits the visitor at each great house. The dedicated individual has at his disposal a whole library of authoritative studies of these places, written by experts such as Christopher Hussey, and lavishly illustrated throughout. It would be presumption on my part to pretend to offer the sort of information contained in those many handsome volumes, even if I had the space in which to do so ; for to write in that vein calls for expert knowledge and the scholar's approach, and in matters such as these I cannot claim to be either expert or scholar.

But I can claim to have visited every one of the houses illustrated in these pages, and many more besides. I travelled to them as (I hope) a visitor of normal intelligence anxious to acquaint himself with something at any rate of the immensely rich architectural heritage of his own country, and also to see some of the priceless treasures to be found in so many of the places visited. I found, incidentally, that many of the great houses (and by no means only the smaller ones) were singularly difficult to locate. I have therefore given rather more detailed instructions for finding them than are ordinarily to be found in books referring to them. Comparatively few are adequately signposted, for it seems that local authorities vary greatly in their willingness to permit specific signposting on their roads. Some of the owners, especially of the smaller places, are inclined, and with reason, to be bitter on the subject.

One important point must be made. On each page there is a note as to opening times. These notes are correct for the year 1969, and many are likely to remain correct for years to come ; but by no means all of them, as I learned on inquiry at each house I visited. In any case, I have omitted the often complicated variations of times-of-opening related to individual months, and distinctions drawn between the hours when the house only, or the gardens only, may be visited. To have included all this detail would not only · have overloaded many of the pages but have been potentially misleading for subsequent years.

There is, however, a way round this problem. Every serious visitor to the seventy-five houses included here (and to the hundreds of others for which space has not been found) will be wise to invest a few shillings in the book mentioned in the opening lines of this foreword. It is published annually by Index Publishers, of London, in the early months of the year ; it can be obtained at most booksellers and news-agents, and very often is among the guide books on sale at the great houses themselves. It will prove an invaluable investment. Its information is up to date, clearly set out, and comprehensive ; it gives dates, days and times of opening for every month ; it tells you how to get there if you have to depend on public transport ; and it tells you whether or not meals or light refreshments are available, either at the house or in the vicinity : a useful piece of information, for sightseeing in some of the larger places can be a tiring and thirst-inducing occupation, however enjoyable and rewarding it may be. To travel round the country with this publication at hand is to ensure that you need never be disappointed or frustrated by arriving on the wrong day, or too early or too late on the right day. In the course of many weeks of driving throughout the length and breadth of England in search of the material condensed into this book, it was my 'bible' and safe-conduct pass.

Garry Hogg,
Groombridge,
Sussex.

Bedfordshire

Woburn Abbey

In Woburn on A50, eight miles north-west of Dunstable

Open daily throughout the year

Everything about this great house is on the heroic scale : three thousand acres of parkland ; art treasures estimated to be worth £5,000,000 ; no fewer than fourteen state apartments ; a unique private collection of wild animals, including rheas, llamas, wallabies, rare species of deer, herds of bison — the list is endless. And the names of the artists whose masterpieces adorn the galleries and state rooms constitute a roll-call of the elect ; Van Dyck, Gainsborough, Poussin, Franz Hals, Velasquez, Rembrandt, Murillo, to mention painters only.

This has been the home of the Russell family for three centuries ; it is still a home, and the resident owners go to some pains to emphasize that they are there to make welcome the thousands of guests who come to absorb something of the great heritage built up over the centuries. You will

be captivated by the strange, probably unique, Grotto Hall, constructed by the fourth Earl and consisting of a myriad of assorted shells, and hardly less by the world-famous collection of Sèvres china presented by Louis XV of France 'for services rendered.' You may remember best the Chippendale furniture in Prince Albert's Dressing Room, or the comparative intimacy of the Yellow Drawing Room, or the spectacular grandeur of Queen Victoria's State Bedroom, with its appropriately gilded ceiling ; or you may be even more impressed by the Flying Duchess's Room, with its mementoes of that remarkable pioneer airwoman who disappeared over the North Sea on a solo flight at the age of seventy-two. In the State Dining Room you may feast your eyes on a literally priceless display of gold, silverware and plate, over-looked by a magnificent Van Dyck portrait above the ornate fireplace. But for some, surely, the enduring memory will be the Canaletto Room, containing more than a score of Venetian subjects serenely beautiful on the white walls above the lavishly appointed great table.

To appreciate to the full the riches and glories to be found at Woburn it would be best, if this were feasible, to visit the place on successive days, and for not too many hours at a stretch, for this is a vast private museum of almost unbelievable variety. But it is also, let it be emphasized, for all its vastness and variety, the home of a Duke and his Duchess who cherish it not only as their country home but as a way of life.

Buckinghamshire

West Wycombe Park

On A40 London-Oxford Road, just west of West Wycombe

Open daily, except Mondays, in July and August

This interesting and in many respects highly unusual house stands in some three hundred acres of ornamental grounds on the south side of the main road to Oxford and is overlooked from the north side of the road by the gentle slopes of the Chiltern Hills. Built a mere two hundred and fifty years ago, it is youthful indeed compared with nearly four hundred older houses scattered the length and breadth of England, from Northumberland to Kent, from East Anglia to Cornwall. But the original builder's son, Lord Despencer, was a member of the notorious eighteenth-century Medmenham Club, more generally known as the Hell-Fire Club, and it is not surprising that, eccentric as he was, he made a good many alterations and even more additions to the structure for which his father, Sir Francis Dashwood (ancestor of the present occupier), was responsible. Notable among these is the Mausoleum on the hill top overlooking the house, designed to accommodate club members, though only he and one fellow-member were buried there.

The grounds afford a good example of contemporary landscaping, and the drive curves among trees to arrive at the imposing west portico. Like many other features of the house and grounds, this bears another and suggestive (or at least unexpected) name : the Temple of Bacchus. All four fronts of this somewhat severe looking house give on to unexpected but characteristic features in the grounds such as the famous Temple of the Four Winds, the Temple of Music and the Temple of Apollo, which also bears a nickname, 'Cockpit', a reminder that in a harsher age cock-fighting took place there. The east (or Great Tuscan) portico is reminiscent of the Italian Palladio and the Corinthian and Ionic columns lend dignity, even austerity to almost the whole of the composition here at West Wycombe.

Within, you may take your choice among the Red Drawing Room, the Blue Drawing Room and the State Drawing Room, all of which have outstandingly fine painted ceilings, notably the last, which is domed and represents the Banquet of the Gods ; the study, with its array of family portraits and the fine mantel mirror which for a time adorned the American Embassy in London ; and the saloon, with its beautiful fireplace of jasper and Siena marble. Classical mythological subjects seem the dominant motif throughout and the many artists employed seem to have given free rein to their talent.

Cambridgeshire

Sawston Hall

On A130 Saffron Walden-Cambridge Road, six miles south of Cambridge

Open at Easter; on Saturdays and Sundays from July to September; on Sundays and Bank Holiday Mondays in May and June

You might miss this charming sixteenth-century manor house if you were travelling too fast along the main road south of Cambridge, for the approach is by a narrow road almost completely shrouded in trees, branching off eastwards from the village of Sawston at the point where the Memorial to the Fallen stands. You should not miss this house, however, for it possesses a quality of intimacy that is often lacking in the larger houses. It is essentially a family house, though it has seen history in the making; indeed it was rebuilt as a royal gift from Mary Tudor to the Huddleston family, after it was burnt to the ground by supporters of Lady Jane Grey; successive generations of the family have lived in the house for more than four hundred years. The fabric of the house is unusual for Cambridgeshire in that it is built of stone.

Not surprisingly, it is firmly believed to be haunted. You may well feel this to be true, especially if you avail yourself of the opportunity to view it in the autumn, when it is lit by candlelight, and great open fires burn in the hearths, accompanied by the sound of sixteenth-century music. But you do not need to be particularly imaginative to see the priest's hole, one of the most remarkable of these features anywhere in the country. Sawston has always been a Catholic family's home, and it is largely for that reason that so much history, often of a violent nature, has been enacted here.

You will find beneath this roof an unexpectedly spacious Long Gallery; and also the Little Gallery, built later than the original fabric in order to by-pass the main bedrooms, and containing a charming Flemish triptych. There is also of course (even if not on a large scale) that essential feature of medieval and Tudor houses, the Great Hall, focal point of the occupants' lives. As would be expected, there is a beautiful chapel. And of course there is fine panelling everywhere, hung with notable pictures and surrounding beautiful and appropriately chosen furniture.

The exterior is as charming as the house itself, with its courtyard and moat and beautifully planned gardens. On the trim lawns, within their periphery of noble trees, guinea-fowl stroll leisurely about, an eye cocked from time to time at the mellow stone and mullioned windows of the modest mansion to which they belong.

Cheshire

Adlington Hall

Off A523 Stockport-Macclesfield road, five miles north-west of Macclesfield

Open on Saturdays, Sundays and Bank Holidays from Easter to the end of September

The ancient Cheshire family, the Leghs, have lived at Adlington for six-and-a-half centuries, and occupy it still. This is one of the county's traditional 'black-and-white' houses. Though details have been altered during the centuries—for instance, a Georgian front was added to the original fabric two centuries ago—it is substantially what it was when it was first built, quadrangular in layout and surrounded by a moat. The immediate impact it makes is similar to that of all massive oak-beam-and-white-plaster buildings : strength coupled with a touch of fantasy. But here at Adlington the sheer weight of the oak is not quite as overpowering as it is, for instance, at Rufford Old Hall or Little Moreton Hall.

Within, the proportions of the various rooms immediately impress, notably those of the fine drawing room, with its 'egg-and-tongue' moulded ceiling, its beautifully executed panelling and mouldings and its Corinthian columns. A Georgian staircase leads to the dining room, with its notable display of family and other portraits. However, it is probably the Great Hall which here, as in so many of our great houses, makes the strongest and longest-lasting impression. It was completed, as an inscription records, as long ago as AD 1505. A remarkable feature of this particular Great Hall is the presence of two massive oak trees supporting the east end; they still have parts of their roots beneath the floor, but have been skilfully carved into octagonal sections from floor level to the lofty ceiling above. Between the pair of oak pillars you may be surprised to find an organ installed; you may be still more surprised to learn that it dates from the seventeenth century and is

held to be the largest and best preserved in the country. Handel himself played on it when he once stayed at Adlington.

There is indeed an immense amount to see in and around this lovely half-timbered mansion. As you wander about, you will be very conscious that the house has always been lived in and so retains a note of domesticity, even of intimacy, in spite of (or perhaps because of) the long centuries that have rolled over it. Do not leave without taking a turn in the gardens and admiring the yew walk and the three-centuries-old lime avenue.

Cheshire

Capesthorne

On A34 Congleton-Manchester road, six miles north of Congleton

Open on Sundays and Bank Holiday Mondays from Easter to September; and on Wednesdays also from May onwards

This is a house conceived and built on the majestic scale, but it ranks among the less ancient of our great houses because the original house on this fine site, after various vicissitudes and much building and re-building, was gutted by fire more than a century ago. So what you see today is the handsome — some might say florid — conception in the Victorian tradition, a status symbol, as it were, of the wealthy owners of that era. You approach it by way of a sweeping drive through parkland, to be confronted by an imposing façade, a great sweep of steps, a dominance (even perhaps a predominance) of turrets and tall clusters of chimneys. Of the original, early eighteenth-century structure only a fragment remains : a little chapel on the south side of the house.

There is a somewhat cold splendour about the interior, with its statues and busts of white marble, its ornate plasterwork ceilings, and the wholly unexpected and anomalous figure of an Egyptian subject three thousand years old which tends to catch and hold the eye even more than the great crystal chandeliers overhead.

In addition to the wealth of fine pictures and the varied and valuable display of notable specimens of furniture in the main rooms, there is a feature of particular interest to overseas visitors, particularly those from the United States of America. Quite recently a portion of the mansion has been given over to what can best be described as Americana. A genuine and it would seem wholly successful attempt has been made here to evoke the spirit and atmosphere of the traditional American Colonial home within the walls of a Victorian home. The essence of this is perhaps captured in the fine example of a grandfather clock from Philadelphia, which will awaken memories in many visitors from the other side of the Atlantic. The inspiration behind this is of course that of the American wife of the present owner, Lt. Colonel Sir Walter Bromley-Davenport. It is quite possible that you may feel, after having explored the vast rooms of this great house, that the note of real intimacy was not struck until you were shown the American room, with its old-fashioned atmosphere, one that will linger in your memory long after you have left the house behind you.

Cheshire

Gawsworth Hall

Off A536 Congleton-Macclesfield road, three miles south of Macclesfield

Open on Wednesdays, Saturdays, Sundays and Bank Holidays from Easter to mid-October

This is a historic place indeed, having been the capital house of the ancient Manor of Gawsworth since the early part of the twelfth century. Many great names have been associated with it, and romantic names, too. Here once lived Mary Fitton, believed by many Shakespearean scholars and others to have been the mysterious 'Dark Lady of the Sonnets'. Here, two-and-a-half centuries ago, the most notable duel in English history was fought : between Lord Mohun and the Duke of Hamilton. And here, too, lived one Samuel Johnson — not the lexicographer but the last of a long line of professional jesters such as Feste and Touchstone ; he was buried in a copse still locally known as Maggoty Johnson's Wood.

This manor house ('great house' seems somehow inapt in this case) is surely one of the most charmingly situated of them all. As you see it today, looking across either the spacious lawns, or the lake, or the courtyard overlooked by the compass window, it is substantially a late-fifteenth-century building, though it was once larger than it is today. But certainly it can never have been more beautiful, and, it is small wonder that there is affection as well as pride in the voices of its owners as they show you its beauties both within and without. At every turn you are conscious that the place is loved and cherished.

You may be surprised to note that the comparatively new is to be seen here in juxtaposition with the ancient : for example a late-sixteenth-century mantelpiece, a Greek bas-relief in marble, and a neolithic axe-head are all to be seen within the confines of the library — one of the most impressive rooms in the whole house. Ceilings, notably in the entrance hall, are low in the medieval tradition ; the Long Hall has its original fireplace, but also a splendid Chippendale mahogany table ; the dining room is virtually unchanged from Tudor days, with a window in it giving on to the chapel ; the same may be said of the beautiful drawing room.

Every room of course has its treasures in statuary, paintings — by Landseer, de Wint, Lely, Morland and a host of other distinguished artists — and *objets d'art*. But for all this wealth of show-pieces you do not feel that Gawsworth is a museum of rarities ; rather that the owners have surrounded themselves for their own pleasure (and ours) with possessions they both value and love.

Cheshire

Little Moreton Hall

On A34, four miles south of Congleton

Open daily, except Tuesdays, from March to October

This may well claim to be the most picturesque of Cheshire's many black-and-white houses, comparable, certainly, with Rufford Old Hall some miles to the north in neighbouring Lancashire, and even more perfect in its setting. You may possibly feel that the sheer weight of its black oak timbers is overwhelming, that the proportion of black to white is unduly heavy; but so perfect is its setting, amid greensward, with the house reflected in its moat, that the eye speedily becomes adjusted to this. The building stands heavily upon its surrounding carpet of turf.

Three generations of Moretons, owner-occupiers for centuries, have worked on this building. It is indeed a composite structure: a massive oak gatehouse range at once gives access to and protects the mansion proper that lies behind it. The upper floors overhang on beautifully proportioned curved and stepped oak beams, as though gable seeks to confide in gable, window to scan window on opposite sides of the forecourt. The windows are so heavily leaded that you may wonder whether any Moreton ever wished to see across the moat that contains the house on all four sides, to the beautiful Cheshire landscape reaching to the horizon beyond. It is unlikely that you will see anywhere else in the country a more complex and impressive assembly of massive oak beams, iron-hard with age, than those that both make and adorn the fabric of this minor hall. Porches and bay-windows, gallery-ends and gables spring outwards above the cobblestones and flagstones at the most unexpected angles to one another; it is small wonder that one of the craftsmen responsible for them left an inscription to the effect that it was by the

Grace of God that he, Richard Dale, Carpenter, wrought these windows. It is small wonder, either, that this has been taken over by the National Trust, to be preserved and maintained in perpetuity.

Inside, it is largely the same story: a mass of intricately conceived, executed and decorated oak timbering in the Porch Room, the chapel, the gallery, the Great Hall (of course) and the withdrawing room. There is an impression of strength, solidity and permanence more usually associated with stone than with timber; the impression can be overpowering at times, but it is compensated for by the sheer beauty and ingenuity of the craftsmanship so consistently in evidence.

Cornwall

Cothele House

Off A390 Liskeard-Tavistock road, three miles south of Gunnislake

Open daily, except Mondays, from April to September; also on Bank Holiday Mondays

Two miles west of Gunnislake a narrow lane branches southwards off the main road, dipping and narrowing continuously, to end in a curving drive that brings you right to the entrance gates of this house, and affords you your first glimpse of the pleasing contrast between cold hewn granite walls and flower-filled gardens flourishing on this west bank of the river Tamar, the dividing-line between Cornwall and Devon. This manor house, built almost exactly five hundred years ago, has survived almost completely intact: a tribute to the material and quality of its building, and to its comparative remoteness. The main buildings enclose a cobbled and terraced courtyard, entered only through a massive gateway. Massiveness in miniature would be an apt description, for though Cothele is diminutive by comparison with many of our castle-like great houses, it can hold its own with them in solidity. Several generations of Edgcumbes, that famous Cornish family, lived within these walls before any alterations or additions were made; the first of these was the impressive north-western tower, of this same eternal Cornish granite, constructed some three-and-a-half centuries ago.

Undoubtedly its most remarkable interior feature is the Great Hall, constructed in 1540 and unaltered to this day. Entering it, you find yourself enclosed by rough granite walls, sketchily plastered, hung with trophies dating back to the days of the Spanish Armada, suits of armour and weapons of many types and periods; an enormous refectory table is laid with a great array of old pewter bearing the Edgcumbe arms, surrounded by chairs and chests and other objects dating back down the centuries. In Sir Piers Edgcumbe's Chapel look especially at the clock: it is the oldest surviving unaltered one in the country, a veteran 'blacksmith's job' of wrought-ironwork with two 90 lb weights, of the prependulum pattern. The clock has no dial, but sounds a bell in the attractive bell-cote to be seen above the battlemented roof.

The other rooms contain many examples of furniture and domestic articles that show how the Edgcumbes lived down the centuries. You will find the best of these in the Punch Room, the Red Room and the White Bedroom. Note especially the tapestries, which have a softening effect on the hard granite of which the whole place is built.

Derbyshire

Chatsworth

Off A623, four miles east of Bakewell, seven miles north of Matlock

Open daily, except for non-Bank Holiday Mondays and Tuesdays, from the end of March until 5 October

This is a house truly in the grand manner: massive, austere, with a forbidding exterior, it matches, you may feel, the severity of the Peak District on whose flanks it was built and extended over four centuries. The first great stones were laid in the mid-sixteenth century; successive generations of Cavendishes – the Dukes of Devonshire whose Derbyshire seat it is to this day – built and demolished and rebuilt as tastes and style changed with the years, calling in architects and craftsmen of international note, including the sculptor Cibber and Tijou, the French genius in wrought-ironwork. The result was inevitable.

The house has accumulated within its spaciously windowed walls what is perhaps the richest treasure-chest on a heroic scale in the whole country (though one Duke at least will challenge this claim). You may even feel overwhelmed by what confronts you, and suffer from a form of aesthetic indigestion. There is so much colour, so great a variety of *objets d'art*, so much sheer weight of demonstrable wealth, that you hardly know which way to turn. As is so often the case, one of the most impressive rooms is the Long Gallery, now the library, with its famous gilded-plaster ceiling. But you may be more impressed by the State Dining Room with its Van Dyck portraits, or the Great Chamber, with its painted ceiling, or the great stairs, with the superb balustrade, a masterpiece by that master craftsman, Tijou; or again it may be the State Music Room, with the *trompe-l'oeil* violin and bow that delights and puzzles every visitor and has accumulated a host of legends about itself. There is virtually no limit to what this great house has to offer the avid visitor.

The famous gardens are different from those surrounding other such mansions in that they were laid out on a slope. This has made cascades and natural fountains a notable feature, and much ingenuity has gone into the incorporating of rocks and natural inclines to produce the unexpected at every other turn. The doyen of these fountains, fed by a reservoir at the top of a hill above the gardens, is named the Emperor: it throws its fantastic jet to a height of three hundred feet. Everything at Chatsworth, it may be said, has been constructed on the majestic scale.

Derbyshire

Haddon Hall

On A6 Bakewell-Matlock road, two miles south-east of Bakewell

Open daily, except Sundays and Mondays, from Easter to September

Leaving the busy main road, you take a winding drive that leads you not only across a three-centuries-old stone bridge but as many centuries backwards in time, it seems, as you come within view of this symphony in stone, at once dignified, gracious and warmly welcoming. It may be said to be every imaginative person's conception of a medieval manor house. And so indeed it is. It is wholly enclosed within a twelfth-century containing-wall; for some four centuries the owners, the Vernon family (you will have heard the romantic story of the elopement of Dorothy Vernon of Haddon Hall), went on building within that containing-wall, successive buildings rising around two courtyards separated by the ancient and historic Great Hall and adjacent chambers; the famous garden terraces were completed a mere three centuries ago.

You might be inclined to think that a place so old might well be in a state of near-decay, if not of complete disintegration. But such is not the case, for the following generations of occupants were fortunate in that the stormier events of history passed them by, leaving them and the fabric unscathed. And for three decades the loving care of the late Duke of Rutland, whose family's country seat this has been for so many generations, has seen to the restoration of those portions of the hall which, as a result of some periods when it was not occupied, had begun to show signs of neglect.

This is a rarely beautiful great house which almost insists that the visitor should pass leisurely through its wealth of beautiful rooms : the chapel, with its mural of St Christopher ; the Banqueting Hall with its exquisite Minstrels' Gallery ; the dining room, with its ornate painted ceiling ; the landing, with its seventeenth century Mortlake 'Senses Tapestries', once the property of Charles I ; the Long Gallery with the unusual windows and fine panelling ; the State Bedroom with its fantastic chimney-breast. But the list is endless : ideally one would visit and revisit at close intervals, so as to retain the atmosphere without becoming satiated. The house is built on a limestone slope, and this gives an added quality to the glorious gardens that encompass it ; in those gardens you may perhaps choose to recuperate from the banquet of beauty you have just enjoyed, before deciding whether to return the same day, or later, to indulge in another leisurely, delighted perambulation.

Derbyshire

Hardwick Hall

Two miles south of A617 Mansfield-Chesterfield road, six miles north-west of Mansfield

Open on Wednesdays, Thursdays, Saturdays, Sundays and Bank Holiday Mondays from the end of March to the end of October

This most beautiful edifice has been aptly described as 'the finest flower of Elizabethan renaissance architecture'. Indeed, as you ascend towards it from the shallow valley below, in which you will have descried it from far away, it seems to be blossoming on the hill top like some huge exotic flower of stone. Nor will you be disappointed as you wind among the trees, upwards, ever upwards, and the moment comes when it bursts upon your view.

It was built in the last years of the sixteenth century, during the final widowhood of its remarkable owner, 'Bess of Hardwick'; her touch is everywhere to be seen and felt, and it is characteristic of her that she should have had her initials inscribed in immense stone lettering along the top edges of the four great square towers that dominate the whole building. In spite of its great size, and the mass of stone it contains, Hardwick Hall somehow contrives to give an odd impression of lightness — perhaps because of its unusually spacious windows on each floor. Indeed, the house almost seems to smile gently down on the visitor looking up at it in wonder and admiration.

Inside, there is a vast array of treasures of many kinds awaiting you. The great Entrance Hall not only extends from the front to the back of the building but rises two full storeys also ; it contains one of the finest chimney-pieces you are likely to find any-where among the great houses of England. It contains, too, some magnificent panels of tapestry, woven in Brussels and hung almost as soon as the hall was completed. Even more magnificent is the High Great Chamber, dubbed by more than one connoisseur 'the most beautiful room in Europe'.

Tapestry was most evidently a passion with Elizabeth, Dowager Countess of Shrewsbury — 'Bess of Hardwick' as she is more intimately known : you find specimens, and superb specimens at that, on every hand. Do not miss, for example, those in the Long Gallery, on the Upper Landing, in the State Bedroom and the Green Velvet Room, to mention only a few. And look out for the many specimens of exquisite needlework to be found in so many rooms : Bess was no mean needlewoman herself. Tapestries and needlework form a satisfying contrast to the grandeur and the nobility of stone staircases, pillars and paved floors, which themselves enhance their intimate beauty.

Derbyshire

Melbourne Hall

On A514 Derby-Ashby-de-la-Zouch road, eight miles south of Derby

Open at Easter; then Whitsun; then daily except Mondays and Fridays throughout the summer months

This most enchanting hall, one of the smaller and more intimate of our great houses, is located at the end of a short cul-de-sac leading from the main road to the Church of St Michael with St Mary; it is in fact so secluded that you could well pass through Melbourne village without being aware of its gracious presence. It is now the country home of the twelfth Marquess of Lothian, a mansion first built early in the seventeenth century, on a site that had already been occupied for four centuries, by Charles I's Secretary of State. A hundred years afterwards a descendant redesigned much of it, giving it its notable classical façade and also laying out the formal gardens which are among its greater glories.

The term 'charming' cannot often be aptly used to describe a great house, but it is appropriate here. The rooms, and much of their contents, give the impression of being on a smaller, more modest scale than those in so many great houses; there is a sense of intimacy wherever you turn – even the portraits here seem less condescending, less severe, than those in many another Long Gallery or state apartment. Not the least pleasing of the rooms you may enter is the ground floor study, in use by the owner when he is in residence and clearly revealing his tastes. On a more ambitious scale is the drawing room, with its impressive array of portraits, its cabinets of priceless porcelain and its Chippendale mirrors; and the library too, with its close associations with Lord Palmerston.

The gardens are among the finest in the 'formal' style anywhere in the country. They were most skilfully and imaginatively laid out two centuries ago in such a way as to take possession, so to speak, of those who walk in them and lead their eyes to the focal points that were their inspiration. Particularly noteworthy is the so-called yew tunnel, earlier than most of the gardens, and emphasizing their general lightness by its strangely effective air of secrecy and sombreness. But it is the Birdcage – a masterpiece in wrought-ironwork by a Derbyshire blacksmith – that draws and holds the eye before and after all else; a miracle of craftsmanship in a formal-natural setting of velvet lawns, flower-beds and the hint of the lake beyond.

Devon

Chambercombe Manor

Off A399, on the outskirts of Ilfracombe

Open daily from Easter to mid-October

This is a house so modest and unassuming that you may feel it just is not worth your while to visit it. If so, you will in fact miss more than you realize. So take the short road that climbs right-handedly off the main road east of the town and then drops steeply between high-banked hedges to end in front of the house of which you will already have caught a welcoming glimpse through the overhanging trees

It lies at the bottom of a cup-like hollow of steeply-sloping turf interspersed with trees : a true Devonshire 'combe', in fact. This siting gives the cluster of buildings of local stone, roofed with heavy slate, a peculiarly withdrawn, intimate, sequestered appearance. And this is as it should be, for there is nothing grandiose, nothing pretentious, about this Devonshire manor house ; it is a manor house in miniature, and might well at first sight be mistaken for an unusually picturesque and well-tended farmhouse. Indeed, for a time it was just that.

Chambercombe started life as a manor house somewhere in the late fourteenth or early fifteenth century ; then it lapsed into being just a Devonshire farmhouse, and was occupied as such for many generations until, under new ownership, it reverted to its former more distinguished status. This is how you will find it today : a charming congeries of modest, low-ceilinged rooms, each a room that has most evidently been lived in and cherished by a succession of owners, both farmers and gentry.

You will pass through a beautiful Tudor doorway, comparatively recently discovered and restored, into the Old Kitchen, with its cider-press and apple-crusher ; through a Gothic doorway into the diminutive private chapel ; into the main bedroom, the Coat-of-Arms Bedroom, with its remarkable wagon-roof ceiling and Elizabethan plaster frieze ; into the Chippendale Room, with its beautiful tallboy and handsome four-poster bed. And so from room to room, often up a step or two and down a step or two, beneath low lintels, back to the Hall, with its foot-square oak beams and its beautiful lime-ash floor, the pride of its owners. And at length into the old-world gardens amid which this charming manor house sleeps so appropriately, girt about with lawns and flower beds beneath the circumambient tree-clad slopes of turf.

Devon

Powderham Castle

On A37, seven miles south of Exeter

Open daily, except Saturdays, from mid-May to mid-September

The gates to this house are in the heart of Kenton village, on your left as you travel southwards from Exeter, overlooked by a gatehouse. The long drive dips, and then rises, through pleasing deer-cropped parkland, to bring you straight to the entrance of the massive castle itself. It was built almost six hundred years ago by the great Devonshire family of the Courtenays; but what confronts you so imposingly today has been considerably restored as a result of the ravages during the Civil War of three centuries ago. Yet you must be something of an expert to detect, as it were, the 'joins', and the over-riding impression you gain is one of strength with grandeur; which is as it should be, for it is a historic castle and at the same time the home of a family proud of a long and distinguished tradition.

The gatehouse and the courtyard by which you will enter the castle date back little more than a century, for it was in the middle of the nineteenth century that the 10th Earl of Devon changed the main entrance from its original site overlooking the wide estuary of the River Exe flowing south into the English Channel from Exeter and the moors to the north of the city. Once within, however, the choice of period is wide, the variety most rewarding, the contents memorable indeed.

There is the great Banqueting Hall, with its traditional Minstrels' Gallery and ornate fireplace; there is the Ante-Room, part of the original medieval building, with its unusual and perhaps puzzling window-fireplace; there is the library, the music room — the latter being a beautiful example of eighteenth-century designing, light and airy, with a fireplace of Carrara marble; there is the famous China Room, adjacent to the library, formerly the medieval Guard Room, with its magnificent display of china, most of it French. And there is, perhaps above all, the glorious Staircase Hall with its superb plasterwork on ceiling and walls. This is rivalled only by the Marble Hall which contains three arches dating back to 1390 even though it was redesigned two centuries ago. Not a single room in this vast place is without its objects of particular and abiding interest; and unlike some great houses of equal stature, this is both museum and a home that has been lived in continuously down the years.

Dorset

Athelhampton

On A35, six miles east of Dorchester

Open on Wednesdays and Thursdays from the end of March to the end of September, and also on Bank Holiday Sundays and Mondays

If you are travelling westwards in the direction of Thomas Hardy's Dorchester (not the town of the same name in Oxfordshire), you will pass through the village of Tolpuddle, with its memories of the Tolpuddle Martyrs, and come almost at once, beneath close-set trees on your right-hand side, to the entrance to this lovely house, said by many experts to be one of the most beautiful, as well as the most historic, of the medieval manor houses in the whole country, not merely in this county of beautiful stone buildings of distinction as well as antiquity.

The house is L-shaped, and it seems somehow to come to meet and welcome you as soon as you have passed through the gate set in the low stone arch that protects the house from the casual passer-by; its noble stone façade rises graciously above the greensward and the gravel of the brief intersecting drive. The building you see is five hundred years old, though here and there judicious alterations have been carried out; but there has been a house, a family home, on the site for more than eight centuries in all. You will not have spent many minutes within its walls before becoming conscious that the place has been cherished by generations of its occupants, and is cherished by them still. The massive walls and sturdy arches speak of resistance to threats from potential enemies; the interior speaks of peace and family life.

You will find countless treasures that are family heirlooms, though they are also museum pieces; they are better seen in this setting than in a museum's glass cabinets. In the Great Hall there is linenfold panelling and a fifteenth-century timbered roof virtually unaltered since it was constructed five hundred years ago. There is another fine timber roof, as well as beautiful panelling, in the King's Ante-Room, from which you pass through Tudor archways into the Great Chamber, or drawing room, where you will see an eighteenth-century harpsichord that once belonged to Queen Charlotte. As might be expected in a house so continuously occupied, furniture is here in abundance, furniture of rare beauty, matching the portraits and tapestries on the panelled walls. But leave yourself time to wander also in the gardens, which form a perfect setting for a medieval house of such graciousness.

Dorset

Forde Abbey

On B3167, off A30, four miles south-east of Chard

Open on Wednesdays from early May to the end of September; and also on a good many Sundays throughout the main summer months

This house is less easy to locate than many, and directions should be followed carefully. Five miles west of Crewkerne, or three miles east of Chard, a minor road, B3167, branches off southwards, dipping into the hollow through which runs the stripling River Axe, bound for Axminster and Axmouth. Take this lane slowly, for it narrows progressively between high banked hedges. These open out unexpectedly, after some three miles, at the entrance gates to this most memorably beautiful former Cistercian Abbey, dating from the middle of the twelfth century.

Only portions of the original fabric remain today – notably the twelfth-century Chapter House, later converted into the chapel, and the thirteenth-century Dorter, or Monk's Dormitory, which is notable for being more than fifty yards long and possessing an engagingly simple yet impressive vaulted ceiling. The Undercroft, too, dates from this period, seven centuries back into our historic past. After the Dissolution, however, major alterations were put in hand. Parts of the Abbey that had been rebuilt in the Gothic tradition were further restyled and absorbed, and the result is a house whose main façade overlooking the ornamental lake, is no less than four hundred feet in length and most satisfyingly proportioned. The stone used in the building of the Abbey, and for the later renovations, is the warm and glowing local limestone which is one of the prime blessings of this largely unspoiled county : it glows even on dull days ; on sunlit days it becomes almost incandescent.

Forde Abbey contains – perhaps surprisingly for a great house so tucked away off the beaten track – one of the most famous of all private collections of tapestries, some of them presented to the eighteenth-century owner by Queen Anne herself ; they are the work of Brussels weavers imported to Mortlake (after which they take their name) in order that English weavers might learn the niceties of the craft.

And these are only a few of the riches to be found within this former abbey. Whether you wander through the rooms, or content yourself mainly with exploring the gardens, you cannot escape being aware of beauty on every hand : a beauty that leaves an indelible impression on the heart and the spirit, as well as on the mind.

Co. Durham

Raby Castle

On A688 Bishop Auckland-Barnard Castle road, one mile north of Staindrop village

Open on Wednesdays and Saturdays from Easter to September

This is one of the most impressive of the great houses even in a part of the country noted for the magnificence of such places, the far north of England. As long ago as the twelfth century it was the home of the great Northern clan of the Nevills; since those far-off days it has been the home of a succession of dukes and belted earls. Probably its most impressive aspect — and it certainly is impressive! — is that which you see as you approach it across the parkland from the southern gateway: no fewer than ten great towers soar into the sky. No two of them are identical in height; they range from the sixty-footer (modestly known as Joan's Tower) to the eighty-footer, highest of them all, Clifford's Tower. Seen across the wide moat, they give an overwhelming impression of strength and impregnability.

Though much alteration was carried out during the nineteenth century, and there were many additions to the original fabric too, there is still a great deal to be seen that is virtually unchanged since the masons began their work on the site in the early years of the twelfth century. The Great Gateway, for instance, known also as Nevill's Tower; the Barons' Hall, with its fine lancet windows; the Rose of Raby Room (a lovely name indeed) inside the ancient keep, one part of the castle hardly touched down the centuries; and the kitchen, a room nearly forty feet in height and still much as it was six hundred years ago; and there are other examples of the kind, besides.

Whether the rooms have been altered, or extended (as in the case of the vast Barons' Hall), or not, they have been gradually filled with treasures in the form of statuary, furniture, notable portraits and so on — all of which have been absorbed into the fabric and atmosphere of Raby Castle so that they are now truly a part of the ancient place. In the dining room look especially at the chimney-piece of snow-white marble; in the Octagon Drawing Room you will be enchanted by the yellow silk wall panelling and the ornamentation of the high vaulted ceiling. The entrance, or Lower Hall, is remarkable not only for its size but for the 'avenue' of octagonal pillars running its full length and marking the eighteenth-century 'carriageway' laid down there in honour of a returning son.

Essex

Audley End House

On A11 Bishop's Stortford-Cambridge road, one mile west of Saffron Walden

Open daily, except non-Bank Holiday Mondays, from April to early October

The original mansion built here in 1603 was so enormous that King James I is reputed to have said to the 1st Earl of Suffolk, who commissioned it, that it was too large for a monarch though doubtless just right for a Lord Treasurer. In sheer extent it far exceeded the vast Hampton Court Palace ; it took thirteen years to build, cost a fantastic sum, and when the owner eventually found it too costly to run, was sold by him to Charles II to serve him as a country palace. Two-thirds of the original mansion were deliberately demolished in the early part of the eighteenth century on the advice of the great dramatist-architect, Vanbrugh. What remains is still palatial.

It lies just off, and visible from, the main road : a magnificent stone façade ornamented by a series of turrets and immediately note-worthy for the splendidly spacious mullioned windows, which appear to rise from ground level almost to the ornate parapet that runs its full length. Two larger towers, and some fine clusters of grouped chimneys, rise behind the façade to break what you may think a severe line.

Within, as you would expect, are state rooms to match the dignity and splendour of the walls enclosing them. In them you will find the work of architects and craftsmen representing several centuries since the initial building. The Great Hall, for instance, with its elaborate screen at the north end, was substantially remodelled in the eighteenth century, the screen being balanced by a fine staircase constructed at the south end. The saloon has one of the most interesting plasterwork ceilings anywhere, with ornamentation that has led to its being called the Fish Room. The drawing room is little more than a century old and contains an outstanding collection of furniture and *objets d'art*, as does the library. Other rooms well deserving careful examination are the Great Drawing Room, the Painted Drawing Room, the Neville Room with its impressive state four-poster bed, and the Adam Rooms with their rich assembly of Adam's masterpieces. Certainly one room you will long remember is the Alcove Room with its richly painted ceiling and the golden pillars supporting the feature that gives the room its name. Indeed, there is so much to see at Audley End that you may well be thankful that, today, it offers but one-third of what it originally had to show.

Essex

Beeleigh Abbey

On a minor road off A414 Chelmsford-Maldon road, one mile west of Maldon

Open on Wednesdays throughout the year

You must persevere in your search for this gem of a place, for it is considerably less easy to find than many. Take the minor road out of Maldon that is signposted Woodham Walter, and after one mile turn off to the right down a lane that ends, in a few hundred yards, at the very gateway of this most beautiful relic of the twelfth-century home of the Canons of the Premonstratensian Order, one of (originally) some thirty-four such monastic houses distributed about this country.

Only part of it exists to this day, but what does remain is of quite extraordinary beauty as well as historical and archaeological interest. Most of the cloister court on the east side survives the centuries : it comprises the vaulted Chapter House, the Calefactory, or Warming House, and the Dormitory above it ; additionally, there are some remains on the south side. To these features were added in Tudor times the portion which catches and holds the eye from the south and south-west ; they form a harmonious whole, for there is the most satisfying combination of mellow red brick and the contrasting, harsher flint, together with half-timbering in the overhanging upper storeys.

What was formerly the Dorter, or Dormitory, now houses one of the most remarkable private collections of books in this country – not surprisingly, either, for the property is now owned by one of the best-known booksellers in the world. But the books and manuscripts are only a small part of the treasures housed beneath this ancient roof. There is much thirteenth-century stained glass ; there is a massive and ornately carved four-poster bed that was specially commissioned to accommodate King James I when he stayed at Beeleigh Abbey. In the Chapter House, which dates from the twelfth century, you can see an organ that was once played on by Handel, and tradition has it that he composed his famous *Largo* on it. In the Calefactory – the one room in which members of this monastic order were permitted to relax and warm themselves in the chill days of winter – there is a magnificent fifteenth-century stone fireplace. And all about you there are friezes and wall-paintings and carvings in both wood and stone. Here then is a house seven centuries old that preserves both the ancient tradition and the belongings of the family that cherish it.

Essex

Hedingham Castle

On B1058, just off A604 Cambridge-Colchester road, four miles north-west of Halstead

Open on Bank Holidays and Tuesdays, Thursdays and Saturdays from May to September

Castle Hedingham is the village above which this enormous castle keep rears its masonry to the skies. You will have seen it as you approach, from many miles away, for it was erected, in the mid-twelfth century, on the highest piece of ground in the district. It contrasts strongly with the village that humbly shares its resounding name, for this is a cluster of half-timbered cottages interspersed with a few larger houses of more sophisticated Georgian mellow brick. They seem to crouch low, as though awed by the soaring menace of this eight-centuries-old Norman keep of uncompromising grey hewn stone towering above its tree-clad mound.

To enter the keep you cross a massive four-arched bridge of great age, the warmth of the brickwork further emphasizing the coldness of the gloomy structure beyond. Drawbridge and portcullis have long since vanished, but immediately you penetrate the ten-foot-thick walls you realize that this was built as a last resort for the castle's occupants when the remainder had fallen to the besiegers. You pass directly into a room designed to house the garrison after it had drawn up the bridge and dropped the portcullis behind the last man through. From this room a spiral stone staircase leads up to the armoury, notable for its magnificent example of a Norman arch. You may have noticed that the spiral is designed 'left-to-right'. Why? Because the defender would be retreating upwards and must have his sword-arm free, while the attacker would be forced to use his left arm as he climbed. Doubtless some professional soldier had his say when the architect planned the details of the keep.

Beyond this is the Great Hall, contained within these colossal walls; beyond that, the gallery, and an upper room where the besieged would try to sleep and where the women and children would find their last place of refuge while their men-folk fought off the attackers below. Little else has changed here so far as the fabric is concerned; but it is more than probable that Aubrey de Vere, Lord Chamberlain of England in Henry I's day, and builder of the castle, would challenge the right of the trees to grow so high on the mound he selected for his stronghold: in his day it was imperative that its garrison should have a wide and unobstructed view in all directions over the rolling Essex plain.

Gloucestershire

Berkeley Castle

**Off A38 Gloucester-Bristol road,
midway between the two towns**

**Open daily, except Mondays, from the
end of March to the end of September**

It is only a matter of a few hundred yards between the teeming north-south highway and the almost unnaturally quiet surroundings of this house, on the edge of a small, virtually lost, village. There can be few great houses older than Berkeley; and there is more than a little truth in its claim to be 'England's most historic home'. For here is a building that has been in continuous, unbroken occupation for between eight and nine hundred years. Its owner-occupier today is a descendant of the man who laid the foundations in the reign of King Henry II, on a site that had had a castle on it (admittedly on a much less magnificent scale) from the time of the Norman Conquest. The Berkeley Castle that you see today is substantially what it was when the masons completed their long task in the second half of the twelfth century. The impression it makes is at once formidable and romantic.

Romantic is a word that should be used with premeditation; it is so used here. The great pile stands almost on the Welsh Border, overlooking the River Severn; it breathes of Border warfare. It is a complex of battlements, gloomy archways, secluded courtyards, twisted chimneys, octagonal towers and turrets, enormously thick walls and ramparts and dungeons deep down within them; it possesses everything, in fact, that the historian, the specialist in medieval history, requires for his satisfaction. It was in this grim castle that Edward II was murdered; there are references to the castle, and to the events that took place in and around it, in Shakespeare's plays.

But within these forbidding walls, half engulfed on one side by a mass of trees and open on the other to the splendour of the terraced grass walks and the expanse of water that mirrors its majesty, there are state rooms that can hold their own with any in the land.

In these, indeed in almost all the castle's rooms large and small, treasures abound, treasures amassed by successive occupants of the castle down the long and vivid eight centuries of its life: for instance the famous Berkeley collection of silver; armour and arms galore; furniture, tapestries, panelling and portraits, walls hung with trophies beneath magnificent vaulted ceilings. The variety, the beauty, the antiquity, the rarity of these things at Berkeley are limitless.

Gloucestershire

Dodington House

On A46 Stroud-Bath road, ten miles north of Bath

Open at Easter, then daily from May to September

The imposing entrance gates stand on the right-hand side of the road (going south), within a few yards of the new roundabout by which the A46 crosses the M4 motorway to South Wales. The first memorable fact noticed when visiting this house is that for almost the whole of the long, serpentining length of the approach drive, beneath great trees casting their wide shadows over rolling, undulating meadows, the house itself remains hidden. Then, suddenly, rewardingly, a glint of bright water to the right and below you ; and immediately thereafter the surprise of the mellow stone mansion as it breaks quite unexpectedly upon your enchanted sight.

Formerly there was an Elizabethan mansion here, but at the turn of the eighteenth century, it was replaced by the architect James Wyatt, whose most outstanding neo-classical masterpiece Dodington House with justice claims to be. The architect had to bear in mind the setting devised by 'Capability' Brown, when he started designing the Regency house confronting you today : a task that called for restraint as well as skill and imagination. But he possessed all these qualities, and the result, as you may see for yourself, was wholly successful.

One family, and one only, has occupied this house for almost four hundred years and you will realize immediately you pass through the splendid portico, with its ten great Corinthian-style columns, that you are entering someone's home. For all its splendour, its display of rare pieces that would not be out of place in a museum, this is a lived-in house, with more than a touch of intimacy even in the grandest rooms. The

Great Library, for instance, contains not only its array of ebony and mahogany book-cases but easy-chairs on a fine carpet, so that the visitor has the impression (as well he might) that the occupants have always been leisured and also interested in books.

Columns abound, notably in the great entrance hall, which has a strongly Roman flavour, severely classical, perhaps, but graciously satisfying in its simplicity and dignity. And – a small item this, admittedly, but oddly revealing – within the portico stands Dodington's private manually-operated fire-engine, the sturdy timbers of its chassis picked out in red and blue and its metalwork a dazzle of copper and brass.

Hampshire

Beaulieu Abbey

On B3054, twelve miles south of Southampton

Open daily from April to October; on Sundays only from November to March

To many prospective visitors this house may connote nothing more than the world famous Montagu Motor Museum and the many and diverse rallies held there year by year. But to the serious visitor, the visitor who is primarily interested in comparing and contrasting the great houses of the land, the Motor Museum, excellent and fascinating as it is, must be of secondary importance. For what is to be seen here, virtually astride the picturesque Beaulieu River just before it debouches into the Solent, is the remains of a Cistercian Abbey founded by King John between seven and eight hundred years ago. A great deal of the original fabric, of course, has vanished; but sufficient remains to show what a splendid house it must have been for that most austere order of monks all those centuries ago.

You may still see the arches of the Chapter House, the Cloisters, the Outer Gate House, or Porter's Lodge, with its impressive Inner Hall; the thirteenth-century Domus, or Dormitory (with the charming implication in its Latin name of 'home'); the great dining hall, formerly the reception hall of the Gate House, where distinguished visitors were welcomed in person by the Guest Master, who led them ceremoniously into the presence of the Abbot himself. Do not content yourself simply with gazing at the treasures displayed in these rooms, and at the portraits on their walls; glance upwards at the beautiful fan-vaulting in, for example, the Inner Hall, which ranks with some of the finest in the country.

This place is something more than an ancient Cistercian Abbey transformed into a museum: it is a home, a place that is lived in, the 'domus' of Lord Montagu of Beaulieu, whose loving and intelligent touch can be detected at every point. He lives there — and who would not, in a place so serenely lovely and with such an expanse of water flowing through and around it? This is an idyllic spot, romantic in the true sense of the word and redolent of tradition. And a good impression of how the tradition has been maintained is to be found in the scale-model of Beaulieu as it used to be. Having wandered through what has survived, turn back to the model and, as it were, fill in the gaps, and learn how splendidly these monastic orders built for themselves and their God all those centuries ago.

Hampshire

Breamore House

Off A338 Salisbury-Ringwood road, three miles north of Fordingbridge

Open daily, except on Fridays and non-Bank Holiday Mondays, from Easter to the end of September

This is an Elizabethan manor house of great beauty, set in the heart of glorious woodland. The site on which it stands has had a building upon it for several centuries prior to the building which you now see : a pre-Norman priory, no less, as a number of Saxon tiles found on the site make evident. And even earlier than this, the site and its environs were almost certainly occupied by a small community whose burial-place was the Long Barrow locally referred to and traditionally known as the Giant's Grave. There can be few manor houses, Elizabethan or otherwise, whose foundations are laid on a site known to prehistoric people. Avebury Manor is another.

The house you see today dates from the 1580's, about the time of the Spanish Armada. It is a many-gabled building : from a vantage-point sufficiently high you can count not far short of a score of them, interspersed with beautifully grouped clusters of chimneys. The impression you gain as you approach from the drive across the courtyard gravel is of warmth and serenity — though the place has known violent death in the shape of both suicide and murder, and has been gutted by fire so that the interior (but happily not the exterior) has had to be largely refashioned. Mellow red brick and stone, against a backcloth of noble trees, usually gives this immediate impression ; and the sense of mellowness, of warmth and welcome, is emphasized as you pass through the main entrance into the main hall.

This is another of the great houses that are truly lived in. Two centuries ago it was bought by an ancestor of the present owner-occupier, Sir Edward Hulse, Physician to King George II, as a gift to his son.

The family and their descendants lived there for more than a century, and were happily spared, together with many of their most valuable possessions, when the house caught fire a hundred years ago. But wandering about its gracious rooms today, you would never know that such a disaster had befallen Breamore, for it has been most skilfully and lovingly restored to its original state, and indeed further embellished and beautified by the descendants of that family who live here to this day.

Herefordshire

Croft Castle

Off B4362, five miles north-west of Leominster

Open on Wednesdays, Thursdays, Saturdays, Sundays and Bank Holiday Mondays from Easter to the end of September

You approach the castle from the tiny hamlet of Yarpole through a magnificent avenue of beech and oak trees ; a gentle approach, almost deceptive, for it opens out suddenly to reveal the beautiful façade consisting of a central gabled portion immediately flanked by two half-hexagonal bay windows rising through three storeys to their crenellated top, the whole façade being flanked in turn by two splendidly proportioned and battlemented round towers, matching two others at the rear corners.

The earliest portions of this fortified manor house (it is not strictly a castle), built as a silent warning to marauders along the Welsh Border, date back to the fourteenth or early fifteenth century, but successive occupants have carried out more than the usual amount of alteration to the original structure. For example, it is hardly more than fifty years since the battlemented central porch, with the great mullioned window above it, was added to the east façade that looks out over a smooth lawn studded with noble trees. But you might well be excused for assuming that all was original Gothic in conception, so skilfully has the work been carried out, and you would need to be an expert to recognize the distinction. A century and a half earlier (when the place was already old), the inner courtyard was converted into a Great Hall, a major alteration which again would be recognized only by an expert. The list of these alterations could be considerably extended.

In the interior the accent is all Gothic. You find this in the library, in the library ante-room, and again in the Blue Room; and yet again as you ascend the fine staircase, with its clustered newel-posts. But there is evidence, too, of the mood of a later period:

Georgian panelling in the drawing room, for instance, and furniture by Chippendale in the dining room; you are now in the eighteenth century.

These alterations have been most skilfully executed; there is no impression of the hybrid. And when you go out into the grounds, among the magnificent oaks and the half-mile-long avenue of Spanish chestnuts planted more than three centuries ago, you will find it hard to believe that such ordered serenity was ever disturbed by Border warfare or the Battle of Mortimer's Cross only two miles away across the grounds.

Hertfordshire

Hatfield House

On A1, in Old Hatfield Town, opposite the railway station

Open on weekdays from 25 March to 31 May; then daily, except Mondays, apart from Bank Holiday Mondays, until the end of September

The road here is narrow and you will be driving slowly when you come within sight of the huge wrought-iron gates through which can just be descried, at the far end of a long straight, climbing drive, one of the truly greatest of England's many great houses, the ancestral home of the Cecil family for three and a half centuries. The magnificent south front which you approach through sweeping parkland has been left untouched since it was built for Robert Cecil in the year 1611; though the overall design was the work of Robert Lyminge, the central block is almost certainly the work of the great Inigo Jones, Official Surveyor of the King's Works.

It would be impossible even in much greater space to outline more than a fraction of the riches contained within this vast palace of a house, where down the ringing centuries royalty have been regular visitors and history has been made by their proud hosts. The state rooms are rarely to be matched in any of the other great houses: they constitute the whole of the central portion of the mansion, and every one of them contains treasures that call for the most leisurely and yet concentrated examination. The Marble Hall is the medieval Great Hall in Jacobean terms, with its screen, its Minstrels' Gallery, tapestries and frescoes; it fills two floors, running almost the full width of the building. The principal reception room, known as the King James Drawing Room, is filled with treasures, many of which are gifts from distinguished visitors to Hatfield from all over the world. The traditional Long Gallery is sixty yards from end to end, and apart from having had its original white ceiling gilded is substantially as it was when it was completed in the early years of the seventeenth century.

In the Great Library there are no fewer than ten thousand books, dating from the mid-sixteenth century up to the present day, their richly tooled leather bindings glowing on the heavy shelves. In the magnificent Armoury you may examine armour worn by Spaniards captured when their Armada was sunk. The carving on the Grand Staircase makes it among the finest specimens of this feature anywhere in the world: connoisseurs will recognize the skill with which Italian Renaissance concepts have been superimposed on traditional English ideas, and the result is a miracle of workmanship.

Kent

Chartwell Manor

Three miles south-east of Westerham, five miles west of Sevenoaks

Open on Wednesdays, Thursdays, Saturdays, Sundays and Bank Holidays from 1 March to the end of November

You do not visit this house in search of antiquity and centuries-old tradition, for it makes no claim to possess these attributes; you visit it in order to enter a country house that is intimately associated with one of the greatest men of this age, the late Sir Winston Churchill. It was his home in the country for more than forty years, and every room in it, every corner of the spacious grounds, is imbued with his presence. He left his mark upon it in material as well as spiritual form: it was he who added to the original fabric the east wing, the portion that contains Lady Churchill's bedroom as well as the drawing room and dining room; and you will find in the grounds samples of his own handiwork in the form of brick walls which he built as one means of utilizing his abundant energy when away from affairs of state. The wall surrounding what used to be the kitchen garden, he laid brick by brick; and he built much of the cottage which was designed for his younger daughters.

Naturally the most intimate memorials of the man and his family are inside. In the library you will see the impressive model of the famous 'Mulberry Harbour', for which he was so largely responsible; in the drawing room is the emblem of France in Lalique glass, a present to Lady Churchill from General de Gaulle, who owed so much to them; in the study (which remains today virtually as it was the last time Churchill used it) you will see his beloved 'working desk', a gift from his children, as well as the great writing desk which formerly belonged to Lord Randolph Churchill and which stands on a beautiful and rare Teheran carpet, a gift from the Shah of Persia. The study, with its many portraits and etchings, was the room most beloved by its owner, and it was on his working desk that he penned much of his matchless prose.

There have been a number of changes in the layout and use of the rooms over the years during which the house was in regular occupation; but what you see today is substantially what was known to, and ordered by, Sir Winston and Lady Churchill in their day. You will admire the curved ceiling in Lady Churchill's bedroom, an unusual feature in a house of this type and period; and you will be fascinated by the way an eighteenth-century spinet has been converted into a show-case for Sir Winston's famous collection of medallions.

Kent

Hever Castle

Off B2026, three miles south-east of Edenbridge

Open on Wednesdays, Sundays and Bank Holidays from Easter until the end of September

Perhaps partly because it is one of the smallest of our great houses, this is one of the most romantically beautiful : a Tudor dwelling-house within the protecting wall of what was originally a fortified farm-house dating back seven centuries. Once the home of the Boleyns, it was seized by Henry VIII after he had had his wife, Anne Boleyn (mother of Queen Elizabeth I), beheaded for not producing an heir, and later handed over to his fourth wife, Anne of Cleves, who lived there for seventeen years. So, as you would imagine, and will certainly feel when first this enchantingly beautiful house bursts upon your sight, the place is steeped in history both romantic and tragic.

The impression is strengthened as you cross the moat and pass beneath the port-cullis in the great Norman arch — a portcullis claimed to be the only timber one still capable of operation — and so into the great entrance hall. Its timber arch and massive beams are genuine fifteenth-century, and it is in this hall that you will find Holbein's famous portrait of the ruthless, much-married Henry Tudor. From the hall you will come in due course to the King's Bedroom, with its fifteenth-century ceiling and panelling and spacious (and much used) four-poster bed, among other intimate relics of the monarch. Do not miss a most unusual, possibly unique, feature : the massive, beautifully wrought and intricate door-lock which Henry VIII caused to be carried about with him wherever he went, so that he could be guaranteed privacy and security when away from his own palaces. It is a most beautiful specimen of the locksmith's art, a museum piece about which much has been written.

You may, however, be more interested in poor Anne Boleyn. Here are many mementoes of her : the ornately carved bedhead, her private Oratory, Holbein's exquisite portrait of her, in the Inner Hall ; and in the Staircase Gallery a head-dress worked by her own hands. Relics such as these may leave a stronger impression even than the instruments of torture in the Torture Chamber, or the magnificent display of suits of armour, examination of which may well send you gladly out into the ornamental gardens which constitute so perfect a setting to this ancient fortified dwelling.

Kent

Mereworth Castle

On A26 Maidstone-Tonbridge road, six miles west of Maidstone

Open on Wednesdays from April to August, and on weekdays in September

You can hardly miss seeing your objective if you look to the left when travelling westwards from Maidstone, for it lies at the end of a short, straight drive beyond a pair of fine ornamental wrought-iron gates, not often is a great house to be descried so easily from a main road. It is more than possible, too, that you may not at first believe that what you are confronted with is what you have come expressly to see.

Mereworth has been referred to as a 'most extraordinary sport' among English country houses, and the phrase calls for explanation. This is emphatically not a typical English country house, small or great; it is in fact an almost exact replica of an Italian country house, the Villa Rotunda at Vicenza, the work of the famous Italian, Andrea Palladio: a deliberate copy by a clever Scotsman, Colin Campbell. Inevitably it looks more than a little out of place, or at any rate somewhat unexpected, here in the gentle Kentish countryside.

You will be struck immediately by the overall symmetry of the place, with its two flanking pavilions, its circular lawn, even the two splendid specimens of cedar that frame the whole. You may be struck by the fact that there are no chimneys: this fact is at once one of the architect's triumphs and secrets. He carried the flues along the ribs that support the great central dome in such a way that the smoke escapes through the central 'lantern' and the symmetry of the building is preserved.

This 'temple-villa', with its huge Palladian portico, is rich in treasures. Look especially at the magnificent painted ceiling, by Sleter, in the card room, and at the Venetian effect in the Long Gallery; do not miss the glorious wood-carving in the salon, or the white marble chimney-pieces in the same room. And do not, of course, fail to look up at the interior of the great dome which dominates the whole, and co-ordinates the symmetry. It is this classic effect which predominates here. You may feel it is at variance with the English tradition; but then this is not intended to be 'English': it is a glowing fragment of Italy deliberately transplanted into the south-east of England, in an age (the early eighteenth century) when the aristocracy admired the 'sober expressions of grandeur' they had seen in Italian cities, and sought to reproduce them here when they returned from the Grand Tour.

Kent

Penshurst Place

At Penshurst, on B2186, five miles north-west of Tunbridge Wells

Open on Wednesdays, Thursdays, Saturdays, Sundays and Bank Holiday Mondays from Easter to the end of September; and also on Tuesdays from July onwards

You may be disappointed at your first sight of this house, beyond the rolling acres of parkland that surround it, for the exterior at least seems to lack the aura of romance, the element of timelessness, you have come to associate with it, having read of its link with that great soldier-courtier-poet, Sir Philip Sidney, distant Elizabethan ancestor of the present Lord L'Isle, VC. The house was already three hundred years old in Sidney's day; it has been the home of one great and distinguished family for more than six hundred eventful years.

Your disappointment, if any, will be swiftly dispelled once you have passed into the interior. Now, truly, you tread on history and are surrounded by the memorial of those who saw history made, helped to make it. Penshurst preserves, within, the very feel of a medieval building. The Gatehouse is four centuries old, no more; but the Baron's Hall dates from AD 1340 and rightly claims to be the finest example of a fourteenth-century baronial hall in the whole country. Note particularly its splendid roof — not of oak, for once, but of the rarer chestnut — and the ten life-size figures representing men and women who worked at Penshurst six centuries ago. Be certain to visit the Solar, the chamber which in every great house of the day was reserved for the ladies to use as a withdrawing-room; it has the slit through which they used to look down on the goings-on of their men-folk in the Great Hall.

Today the Solar is the State Dining Room. From it you may pass into the Tapestry Room, with its early sixteenth-century French and late seventeenth-century Flemish master-pieces. In the ancient Crypt you will see a magnificent display of arms and armour, from renaissance times to the State Sword presented by Malta to Lord Gort. And — a more touching relic — in the hall is the helmet carried at Sir Philip Sidney's funeral almost four centuries ago. Not the least notable feature at Penshurst is the Long Gallery (designed for exercise in inclement weather), unusually lit by windows on three sides; it was planned by Sidney's younger brother before the end of the sixteenth century, and its panelling belongs to that distant date.

Kent

Walmer Castle

Off A258 Dover-Deal road, two miles south of Deal

Open all the year round, every day of the week, including Sundays

For two and a half centuries this castle, one of a series of fortresses built by Henry VIII for the purpose of coastal defence, has been the official residence of the Lords Warden of the Cinque Ports — Hastings, Romney, Hythe, Dover and Sandwich. Among those who held this honourable post, and therefore made this their residence for longer or shorter periods, are William Pitt, Lord Granville, and the Duke of Wellington, who died there in 1852 after holding the post for almost a quarter of a century.

You approach it from the main road through a pleasant little park, with which its grim entrance and looming, massive walls constitute an almost violent contrast. Immediately beyond the drawbridge spanning the moat you find yourself beneath a stone archway, above which is a line of eight 'murder-holes' — holes cut vertically through the stone lintel so that boiling oil or molten lead could be conveniently precipitated upon the heads of any who sought unlawful entry. Once beyond the forbidding portcullis, you may speculate as to whether you will ever emerge from this series of concentric bastions with their enormous flanking drum-towers. For this is a fortress built for defence against determined attack from the English Channel, and nothing could be left to chance. The array of offensive weapons is formidable, and you are constantly made aware of the purpose for which this fortress was built.

Yet there are some portions of it that possess at least a hint of comfort, almost of intimacy. There is Pitt's Room, which the Prime Minister once used as a study ; there is Queen Victoria's Room, with its expansive view seawards across the ramparts ; there is the dining room, with its windows of mauve glass, inserted by Lord Liverpool, in his Wardenship, because of his wife's weak eyesight. There is Wellington's Room, which still contains the armchair in which he died and the narrow camp-bed he used on his campaigns and afterwards, Spartan-like, still preferred to any other. You will see his coat, worn when he was Lord Warden, and the original 'Wellington' boots to which he gave his illustrious name. Nor should you forget, when looking at these relics, that the late Sir Winston Churchill, though he preferred his country seat of Chartwell, was installed here in 1946 as Lord Warden of the Cinque Ports.

Lancashire

Rufford Old Hall

On A59 Liverpool-Preston road, five miles north of Ormskirk

Open on weekdays, except non-Bank Holiday Mondays, from April to September; and on weekdays, except Wednesdays, from October to March

This great half-timbered manor house was built in the latter part of the fifteenth century and with some justification claims to possess the finest preserved example of a timbered Great Hall in the Lancashire tradition dating back to Tudor times. As you gaze upwards at the magnificent hammer-beam ceiling you will not feel that there is anything exaggerated in the claim. The Great Hall today is just as it was when it was built. It represents the medieval tradition in Great Halls in that its length is twice its breadth, it has the High Table at one end, adjacent to what was the lord of the manor's private quarters, and the entrance-screen at the lower end.

It is possible that as you examine the interior of the Great Hall and of other rooms, just as when you were first confronted by the exterior as you emerged from the trees that shade the curving drive, you may feel that the proportion of black to white, of massive oak beam and cross-beam to intervening white plaster, is unduly great. But here, as is the case all through Cheshire and down the Welsh Border to the south, you are in 'half-timber country', where splendid and appropriate use was made of the fine oaks growing then in such profusion. The same impression is made by Little Moreton Hall, a few miles to the south. The eye readily accustoms itself.

For centuries Rufford Old Hall was the home of the great Lancashire family of the Heskeths. Thirty years ago, Lord Hesketh gave the place to the National Trust, who will preserve it in perpetuity. Six centuries before that, an ancestor of Lord Hesketh's fought at the Battle of Crécy: his is a long and distinguished tradition. Indeed, tradition here is the keynote. The Hall is redolent of it. And by a most happy stroke of imagination it now houses a museum devoted essentially to objects of local interest: a 2,000-year-old dug-out canoe found in the district; flint axe-heads and spear-heads of bronze; domestic utensils dating back over the near and far centuries; samplers, puzzle-jugs, frogs-in-mugs, horn beakers, and countless other objects locally made, locally in use down the years. All this adds up, you will find, to an intimate impression of life 'above-stairs' and 'below-stairs' in a great house of outstanding quality and atmosphere.

Leicestershire

Belvoir Castle

Between A52 Grantham-Nottingham and A607 Grantham-Melton Mowbray roads, seven miles west of Grantham

Open on Wednesdays, Thursdays, Saturdays, Sundays and Bank Holiday Mondays and from Good Friday to the end of September

From its plinth of close-set trees on a great natural mound this towering mass of battle-mented and heavily turreted masonry dominates the undulating and relatively low-lying countryside; it somehow gives the impression (though on a majestic scale) of a German *schloss* set on a hill-top somewhere in Bavaria. There has been a castle on this commanding site since the Norman Conquest, though the present one, the third to be built here, dates back only a century and half. This largely accounts for the 'Baronial Gothic' style characterizing the exterior, and some parts of the interior.

The immediate impact of the interior is equally formidable – you might almost use the term 'menacing'. You enter by way of the porch and entrance passage, a chamber whose walls are fitted with arms and armour sufficient for a hundred men-at-arms. Thence you pass into the aptly named Guard Room, where you find yourself surrounded on all sides with further specimens of arms and accoutrements, including a remarkable pattern of swords radiating outwards from the Duke of Wellington's medallion like the gleaming spokes of some armourer's wheel. Possibly with some relief you move on to the ballroom, with its portraits which look down somewhat unexpectedly on a sequence of show-cases containing some very gruesome exhibits indeed.

On a less grim note, there are treasures to be found in room after room beyond these: for example in the Chinese Rooms elaborately hand-painted silk hangings, lacquer and exquisite bed-coverings; in the memorable Elizabeth Saloon panelling and an elaborately designed ceiling, a Tournai carpet and an Italian marble fireplace; and a superb ceiling in the Grand Dining Room. There is the Stuart Bed, the Agate Vase, and the world-famous collection of miniatures appropriately housed in the Picture Gallery. And when you have seen all this, and as much again, and again, you have still seen but a tithe of the treasures accumulated beneath this ample roof spanning the country seat of the Dukes of Rutland. But it may still be the actual siting of this great castle-mansion that leaves the strongest impression, and it is appropriate that its very name 'beautiful view' should hint at this. This great house stands poised above a landscape that has gratified the eyes of its successive owners for five whole centuries, and does so still.

Leicestershire

Stapleford Park

Off B676, five miles east of Melton Mowbray

Open at Easter; then on Wednesdays, Thursdays and Sundays from early May to the end of September

You leave the main road and take a small, undulating road, over a bridge and beneath some trees, which open out to reveal the wide entrance gates and twin lodges through which you pass, up a tree-embowered drive to the house itself. Perhaps the most interesting thing about it is that it offers so many examples of work characteristic of different periods in its fabric. Some may be inclined to feel that its most rewarding aspect is the earliest: the Tudor wing built as long ago as the early sixteenth century and lovingly preserved and (where necessary) restored to as close an approximation of its original state as possible. There were alterations and additions too in the early part of the seventeenth century, and again in the latter part, almost exactly three centuries ago. And there were yet more extensive alterations, after the great Robert

Adam, in the mid-eighteenth century. Finally, the south front may correctly be styled Victorian. You might reasonably suppose that the result would be a hotch-potch; yet this is not by any means so, and there is no impression of disunity in the façade and outbuildings that confront you.

The interior proves to be generally less ornate than is so often the case in these great houses; indeed, you might almost say that simplicity is the welcome keynote. Yet you will speedily become aware that there is too much treasure in evidence for the word to be apt. There is plenty of evidence of discretion, taste and loving care in the arrangement of the treasures on display against their lovely settings: in the Long Gallery, for instance, with its exquisite candelabra; in the Big Dining Room, with its beautiful plasterwork and portraits; and not least of all in Lady Gretton's Sitting Room, where you will at once be conscious of the unmistakably feminine, even intimate, touch.

If you have a taste for history — and who can help that, in such surroundings? — you will want to examine the sculptures and stone figures that abound, each of which has a story to tell. And you will certainly not want to leave Stapleford Park without wandering in the park and looking at the bird sanctuary with its rare collection, among other birds, of Canada geese.

Lincolnshire

Gunby Hall

On A158 Horncastle-Skegness road, eight miles north-west of Skegness

Open on Wednesdays, Thursdays, Fridays and Bank Holidays from April to October

The entrance to this charming building lies close to the roundabout on the main road, two miles or so to the west of the village of Burgh-le-Marsh. A black-and-white lodge marks the beginning of a drive through an avenue of limes cleaving parkland in which cattle graze. The house itself stands on a slight eminence at the end of the drive : a façade of plum-red brick, very well windowed, within a framework of well-matched stone. The façade itself seems to exude an atmosphere of serenity ; indeed, it may well be this very building, not yet much more than two hundred and fifty years old, that inspired Tennyson's much-quoted line, 'A haunt of ancient peace'. The Poet Laureate had his home near here, at Somersby, for many years.

Though the house is, in contrast with many in the country, relatively young, it has been owned by one family, the Massingberds, who have lived hereabouts since Saxon times ; indeed, the widow of Field-Marshall Sir Archibald Montgomery-Massingberd makes it her home to this day. And small wonder, either, as you will undoubtedly agree when you have fallen willing victim to its graciousness and charming ambience.

It has been added to over the years, yet such was the skill of the successive architects and builders employed that nowhere is there any hint of misfit or fault in taste and execution. Gunby Hall is well integrated, an harmonious whole. You may never be fortunate enough to see a finer example of the architecture of the period of William III : the brickwork is particularly pleasing, both in its proportions and in its tone, and some of it may have come from neighbouring Holland, though probably the greater part of it came from clay beds in the vicinity. This is, after all, brick country rather than stone. But the stonework of the house emphasizes the mellow beauty of the bricks used, from wherever they may have come.

The interior exercises a beneficent influence on the visitor. It soothes ; it is quiet, unhurried, redolent of memories of those who lived here for generations, whose portraits hang on the walls above the fine furniture, interspersed with portraits of the great of the eighteenth century, of Dr Johnson and his circle, which have been bequeathed to the owner of the house. 'An English home . . . all things in order stored, a haunt of ancient peace' : how accurately, how truly, the poet described Gunby Hall.

Norfolk

Blickling Hall

On B1354, two miles north-west of Aylsham

Open on Wednesdays, Thursdays, Saturdays, Sundays and Bank Holidays from May to 5 October

Once well clear of the attractive little town of Aylsham the road narrows and dips among trees. It will repay you to take this gentle descent very leisurely, looking out for a small church secluded among the trees to your right. Immediately beyond this, the road widens and you find yourself opposite the gates of the Hall. The impact of this most beautiful Jacobean mansion of rose-red brickwork soaring above meticulously maintained lawns on either side of a short central drive is quite overwhelming, at any rate if you have not been to some extent prepared for what you will find. Yew trees of great antiquity (older, certainly, than the house itself) lead the eye towards this nobly windowed façade, turreted and multi-gabled, with its clustered chimneys symmetrically disposed among them. Few great houses of this period, and in this lovely, warm, indeed glowing material, are capable of making such an immediate and such a lasting impression on the visitor.

There has been a manor on this site for nine hundred years and more, but the house that you see there today dates back only three centuries and a half — about the same length of time as the far larger Hatfield House has stood on its Hertfordshire site. Indeed, if you already know Hatfield you may well be reminded of it as you walk up the drive towards Blickling Hall, for it was designed by Robert Lyminge, architect of the Hertfordshire mansion. And once inside, when you study the superbly carved Grand Staircase, you will find an echo of that other Grand Staircase almost certainly the work of the same artist-craftsman.

There have been alterations since Blickling Hall was first built : for example, the original Eating Room was redesigned a century and a half after it was built, and is now the South Drawing Room.

The state rooms are all on the first floor, each a splendid room in its own right, and contributing to the glory of the whole. Here you will find portraits by such artists as Van Dyck and Gainsborough, and a lavish display of tastefully selected and finely preserved antique furniture, as well as tapestries from Russia and wallpapers from China. Both inside and out, this is a rich storehouse of beauty and tradition. As you walk reluctantly away down the drive, between the lawns and enormous yew hedges, look back at the house once more : from midday onwards the whole beautiful façade seems incandescent in the afternoon sunshine.

Norfolk

Oxburgh Hall

On a minor road between Stoke Ferry, on A134, and Swaffham, on A47, some seven miles south-west of Swaffham

Open on Bank Holidays, Wednesdays, Thursdays, Saturdays and Sundays from Easter to 5 October

It is comparatively rare, these days, to come across a small manor house that possesses a moat. Hever, in Kent, is one ; Little Moreton Hall, in Cheshire, is another ; but they are rare. It would be a pity, then, to miss this one when you are in East Anglia, for it is a gem of its rare kind. You will find it if you persevere along an unpromising minor road, on the outskirts of the hamlet of the same name (though spelt Oxborough on map and sign-post). It is the treasured home of the Bedingfelds, an East Anglian family that can trace its line back to the Norman Conquest.

The outstanding feature of the place is undoubtedly the magnificent late fifteenth-century gate-tower of brick that rises no less than seven storeys from the moat that washes its feet. It has withstood time, weather and assault for almost five hundred years, and looks even at close quarters good for as many yet to come. By a most fortunate chance this gate-tower was spared the alterations that took place during the eighteenth and nine-teenth centuries, when, for example, the ancient drawbridge was replaced by a fixed bridge over which you pass into the interior courtyard today, the original Great Hall and kitchens and much of the south-west portion of the house were demolished and reconstructed, and the square tower in the south-east corner was added. Nevertheless, the structure has largely retained its homo-geneity, and the newer brick and stonework blend happily with the older. The windows in the portions that flank the gate-tower may seem just a trifle small for the area they are called upon to light, but immediately above the archway is a magnificent eight-light window that admits sunshine into the King's Chamber, and a six-light window immediately above it that performs the identical function for the Queen's Chamber.

In both these state chambers (the first so named after Henry VII slept in it), in the Great Hall and elsewhere there are fine specimens of armour, leather-bound travelling chests, tapestries, needlework and other examples of domestic property, emphasizing the lived-in aspect of the manor house. But it must be the great central gate-tower that you will remember longest, with its almost unique cut-and-rubbed-brick spiral staircase and finely wrought hand-rail of the same improbable material.

Northamptonshire

Burghley House

Off A1, the Great North Road, one mile east of Stamford

Open on Tuesdays, Wednesdays, Thursdays and Saturdays from 30 March to 5 October and also on Bank Holidays, Good Fridays, and Sunday afternoons

Though several of its imposing entrance gates abut on to the main road, you cannot see this enormous mansion, rightly referred to as 'the largest and grandest monument of Elizabethan architecture', through them or over any part of the otherwise unbroken seven-mile-long perimeter wall. To enter the grounds at all you must take the small road signposted Barnack, which branches eastwards just south of the old bridge below the town. Two miles along this, skirting the great wall, you will eventually come to the entrance to this magnificent home of the Marquess of Exeter. Founded by Elizabeth I's Lord High Treasurer in 1552, it has been the home of the famous families of the Cecils and the Exeters for well over four centuries. But there was a monastery on the site four centuries earlier than that : small wonder, therefore, that the whole vast edifice and its glorious circumambient acres are redolent in history. Much of this, incidentally, can be taken in almost at a glance in the Goody Runkin Room, opposite the Porter's Lodge, for this has been transformed into a museum of archives.

The state rooms, too, have arresting names : the Green Damask Room, the Marquetry Room, the Pagoda Room, the Purple Satin Bedroom, the Heaven Room, are some of these. With many others, they are noteworthy for their magnificent ceilings, frescoes and furniture. It would almost seem that every great artist, every great craftsman over four centuries, has left his signature within these ancient walls. For many it will be the double hammer-beam roof of the Great Hall, no less than sixty feet high, almost as high as it is long, that will be the most memorable feature ; for others it may

be the glorious Painted Staircase, built of Ketton stone ; for others again it may well be that the Old Kitchen will remain the most abiding memory. In addition to its array of no fewer than two hundred and sixty kitchen utensils, it has a spit capable of roasting an ox whole — a task it has undertaken times without number in the past, and could still perform. It will be found in the oldest part of the house, an integral part of the life of the place that, in other great houses, is rarely open to view. So rich in treasures is Burghley House that a bare catalogue of its contents runs to nearly fifty pages ; to describe them fully would demand ten times that number.

Northamptonshire

Castle Ashby

Off A428 Bedford-Northampton road, six miles east of Northampton

Open at Easter ; then on Thursdays, Saturdays and Bank Holidays until the end of September, and additionally on Sundays from June until August

There was a castle on this site seven centuries ago, but the present enormous mansion, not in fact strictly a castle at all, dates back only to the early part of the seventeenth century — late Elizabethan or Jacobean. It carries a good deal of evidence that that incomparable artist-craftsman, Inigo Jones, exercised an influence on its designers and builders. An unusual and striking feature becomes discernible if you raise your eyes three storeys to the balustrade running the full length of the main façades, notably that overlooking the main garden ; you will see that the stonework spells out in great capitals, and in severe Latin, the sentiment that if God does not protect the house the labourers who built it will have laboured in vain.

You approach this house through parkland of spectacular and noble beauty, landscaped — as you will probably have guessed — by 'Capability' Brown and beautified by long avenues of splendid trees planted two centuries and more ago. Indeed, so alluring is the parkland that you may be almost reluctant to leave it for the interior of the house ; but this would be a mistake, for great treasure awaits you within.

Because the place was added to and altered, so far as the interior is concerned at intervals down the centuries, you will find yourself confronted by a variety of styles of ornamentation and design generally. There is the glorious Big Hall, with its noble Gothic timbered roof and its oriel window that gives on to the courtyard beyond. There is the Dutch Wedding Room, with its seventeenth-century Flemish tapestries. There are, in fact three drawing rooms here, severally named the End, the Middle and the Chinese Drawing Rooms, each with its individual art treasures, its portraits by Hoppner and Reynolds and other great artists. As so often in these great houses, the staircases are an important and memorable feature. Here there are two : the elaborately carved East Staircase and the even more sumptuously ornamented West Staircase ; both are objects of dignity and beauty quite apart from their functionalism. And they lead you to the Long Gallery, with its notable collection of Greek vases, one of the finest private collections in the whole country, and the pride and joy of the owner, the Marquess of Northampton.

Northamptonshire

Sulgrave Manor

On a minor road, eight miles north-east of Banbury

Open daily, except Fridays, all the year round

This most charming manor house does not, so far as mere size is concerned, qualify for mention among the great houses, let alone the 'stately homes', of England : it is on altogether too modest a scale for this. But if mellow beauty and tradition be the criteria, then it comes splendidly into its own. For this sequestered house, on the borders of Northamptonshire and Oxfordshire, stands on the site of a much older house, one mentioned in Domesday Book, in the eleventh century.

The house confronting you today, however, was built by a north countryman named Lawrence Washington, rather more than three centuries ago. Washington ? That name strikes a note, surely ? Of course : this north country Washington was a remote ancestor of the first President of the United States of America, George Washington himself. That is why, more often than not, you will find the Stars and Stripes flying over the beautiful stone-slab roof ; and why not, indeed ? The house and grounds were presented by a group of patriotic British subjects to the peoples of Great Britain and America in celebration of the century of peace that had existed, by 1914, between them.

In this quiet village, in the church as well as in the manor house, you will find many memorials to the builder, George Washington's English ancestor. And in the actual house, as you might expect, a wealth of relics and memorials. You will find George Washington's favourite chair, his liquor-chest of oak, his saddle-bags, his velvet coat, even a lock of his hair. But in the main, of course, this essentially English house contains what is traditionally English. You will find in the Great Kitchen a wealth of utensils, an enormous fireplace with three separate ovens, spit-jack and pot-crane. Washington's chair, in the Chintz Bedroom, is the work of the English craftsman, Hepplewhite ; the Oak Parlour has fine panelling and a walnut settee covered in contemporary English *petit-point* needlework ; the Great Chamber has an unusually fine oak-slab floor and a double-framed, high-pitched ceiling. Though this place is no longer fully lived in, it contrives to convey the feeling, to possess something of the atmosphere, of one that is ; a note of intimacy pervades the whole, and leaves you with a warm memory when you take your departure.

Northumberland

Alnwick Castle

On A1, on the north side of Alnwick town

Open daily, except Fridays and Saturdays, from the end of April to the end of September

Alnwick is one of the great Border castles, the most impressive of them all. It has been the home of chieftains constantly at war with the Scots on the indeterminate border not so many miles to the north, the northern seat of the great clan of Northumbrian earls, the Percies, whose name runs through a host of Border ballads and rings in the pages of Shakespeare. The moment you enter Bailiffgate, on the northern exit of the town, you are set about with vast stone walls, with gatehouses and barbicans, with towers and turrets and keeps and battlements which induce an immediate sense of involvement in stirring and bloody historical events. These massive outer walls and the keep date back almost nine centuries; so solidly were they built that for centuries the Scots hammered on them in vain, though they could demolish the lesser (but still massively built) pele-towers along the Border like so many packs of cards. Great stone figures, more than life-size, dominate the battlemented mass of the barbican, and you might think that this is a place where nothing but war and rumour of war could be acceptable. But on this point you would be very wrong indeed.

Pass through the gatehouse and barbican, through the outer and middle bailey, the Constable's Tower and the Postern Tower, and you come at length to the treasures within. They are housed in such chambers as the music room and library, the State Dining Room and the Red Drawing Room — names which seem at first out of place in so menacing a mass of masonry. Here are rare objects on display, the work of artist-craftsmen from many parts of the world, accumulated down the more peaceful centuries by a succession of Northumbrian earls and given an appropriate setting. By no means the least interesting of the contents of this great fortress is the museum recently opened in the Postern Tower to house a remarkable collection of Roman, Saxon, and other relics that, somehow, you would not immediately associate with Alnwick Castle.

Beyond the fortress spread the undulating acres of timbered parkland, to the serpentining length of the River Aln. The contrast between this serenity and the austere fabric overlooking it leaves an impression that will be slow to fade; grim history, you may feel, has only just been overlaid by slopes of kindly turf.

Nottinghamshire

Newstead Abbey

On the A60 Nottingham-Mansfield road, nine miles north of Nottingham

Open daily from Good Friday until the end of September

Eight centuries ago this so-called Abbey – strictly speaking it should be called Priory – was built by Henry II to house a community of Canons Regular of the Order of Saint Augustine ; tradition holds that the gesture was made by the king in expiation of the crime of the murder of Thomas à Becket. The Canons occupied Newstead for almost four hundred years. As you approach it, between the massed trees on either side of the drive, you may be tempted to think there is nothing more to be seen today than the ruined walls of the Priory Church. But in fact, adjacent to this is the Tudor mansion which incorporates so much of the older edifice and now offers a good illustration of what a great house erected on a priory site could become.

Newstead is inseparably associated with the name of the poet Byron, and in fact it was for many years the country seat of the Byron family. You will see their coat of arms, together with the date 1631, on the porch marking the entrance to the east side of the house. A more intimate, and certainly touching, relic of the last member of the Byron family to occupy Newstead is to be found near the site of the original Priory Church. It is the simple but expressive monument erected by the poet to the memory of his beloved Newfoundland dog, oddly named Boatswain, and stated by his master to be the only true friend he ever possessed.

As you would probably expect, there is a certain austerity about the interior, as well as the exterior, of this priory turned mansion. Ruined walls stand side by side with what used to be the living-quarters of a succession of lay occupants, not all of them by any means happy men and women. There are treasures within, on the grand scale : the great tomb of the Byron who died in 1603 ; Thomas Phillips's classic portrait of the poet, painted in 1813 ; the Fraser Collection, the Goodlake Collection and the Roc-Roe Collection. And, on a more personal note, the original manuscript of Byron's verse on the oak tree he planted in the grounds of his home, the four-poster bed and other furniture that he used while up at Cambridge and also at home. Here history is well accommodated and all-pervasive. The sense of timelessness will impress itself upon you the moment you pass the famous Pilgrim Oak.

Oxfordshire

Blenheim Palace

In Woodstock, on A34, eight miles north-west of Oxford

Open on Mondays, Tuesdays, Wednesdays and Thursdays from the end of March to the end of July; then daily except Fridays to the end of September then as before to the end of October

Appropriately enough, this great house is not Blenheim House but 'Palace'. It is of course indelibly associated in all our minds with the late Sir Winston Churchill, who was born here, and insisted that he should be buried in the graveyard of the little church of Bladon, a stone's-throw away from this vast agglomeration of buildings set in a huge parkland with ornamental lakes and elaborately formal gardens.

In contrast with, for example, Berkeley or Alnwick or Montacute, Blenheim is a newcomer, an upstart: the great Vanbrugh was chosen by the then Duke of Marlborough (the place is owned by his descendant to this day) to act as his architect, and work was not actually begun on the site until the early years of the eighteenth century. Why 'Blenheim'? The house was a gift from Queen Anne in gratitude to John Churchill, Duke of Marlborough, for his victory over Louis XIV of France ; Parliament voted towards the project what amounted (fortunately for the Duke) to a blank cheque.

The result of this munificence is what confronts you today : a mansion-palace on the heroic scale, no expense having been spared, for Blenheim was designed to be something more than a home worthy of a deserving hero ; it was to be a National Monument to the glory of the country that had, under Marlborough's inspired leadership, triumphed over her traditional foe. Including an interval when both materials and skill ran short, the Palace was some seventeen years in the building. Nor does this surprise as you wander through its vast state rooms or survey its glorious façades from the limitless acres of parkland in which

it is set – parkland, once again, that owes its character to the genius of that ubiquitous figure, 'Capability' Brown.

And what should you look for especially ? There is an *embarras de choix*, here. Perhaps the famous Rysbrack tomb in the Chapel ; or perhaps the sixty-yard-long Long Library, with its wonderful ceiling ; or again, perhaps the murals in the saloon. But indeed the choice awaiting you is infinite, both within and without these splendid walls. You may even remember best the room, to the west of the Great Hall, in which on 30 November, 1874, Winston Churchill first saw the light of day.

Oxfordshire

Rousham House

Off A423 Oxford-Banbury road, twelve miles north of Oxford

Open on Wednesdays and Bank Holidays from June to August

To locate this place you should turn eastwards off the main road between Oxford and Banbury at a crossroads marked by the Hopcroft Inn. Your road dips between trees, narrowing as it dips, to open out just short of a picturesque bridge spanning the Cherwell. You turn right before crossing the bridge and come almost at once to the gateway giving access to a drive that in fact leads past the house to the tiny hamlet of the same name. Rousham itself stands up boldly on your left. Essentially it is Jacobean, dating from the first half of the seventeenth century; but to its Jacobean core much has been added over the centuries, notably the two great wings that were built rather more than a century after the original building. If you look carefully you will see an eloquent memento of the earliest period: in the oak door of the entrance hall you can discern the holes through which the first owner, Sir Robert Dormer, had his men-at-arms train their muskets on any Parliamentarians foolish enough to approach within striking distance; they tell their own story.

The staircase, too, is Jacobean, as is the Oak Chamber, a room which survived the elaborate alterations carried ruthlessly through by William Kent in the first half of the eighteenth century. Kent's impress is probably seen at its most emphatic in the room known as the Painted Parlour, where the ceiling consists of an elaborate painting of arabesques and a central medallion containing a group of mythological figures done on canvas by Kent himself. But it is the Great Parlour which will probably impress itself most strongly on the visitor; this was originally General Dormer's Library and has a strong note of what has been referred to as 'Kent Gothick' — a not entirely happy admixture of the classical and the Gothic traditions.

Kent was also responsible for the elaborately designed gardens, which he laid out with his eye on the River Cherwell at their foot. Good use was made by him of the water available, and certainly Venus's Vale and Kent's Arcade justify the claim that this is the finest example of his landscape gardening. From the gardens can be descried, high on a neighbouring hill, the odd Folly known as 'Kent's Eye-Catcher'; but this, unlike his interiors and exteriors, is something of a monstrosity.

Shropshire

Stokesay Castle

On A49 Shrewsbury-Ludlow road, seven miles north-west of Ludlow

Open daily, except Tuesdays, throughout the year

There is probably no finer example of a fortified manor house — it is not strictly a castle in the accepted sense of the word — to be found anywhere in England. You will be struck immediately by the curious juxtaposition of half-timbering and solid stone ; oddly enough, it is the gatehouse by which you enter the courtyard that is the half-timbered portion, not built of hewn stone, as you would naturally expect. It has been dated to the early years of the seventeenth century, and is thus almost of the period of such half-timbered buildings found in Cheshire and Lancashire. In the old days a moat surrounded the place, with a bridge to give access to the gatehouse.

From the gatehouse you pass immediately into a walled courtyard, on the far side of which stand the massive stone buildings that constitute the castle itself : a block used for living-quarters, flanked by two impressive towers. This portion of Stokesay dates from the early part of the fourteenth century — three hundred years earlier than the gatehouse. An imposing feature of these stone buildings, the original Great Hall and the Solar, is the array of stepped buttresses that brace them between gable and gable, as do their even more impressive counterparts at the corners of the south tower. The north tower, incidentally, has not four but five sides, and dates from about the year 1300 : it looks good for at least a further seven centuries. Even the unusual and unexpected timberwork on the exterior of the upper storey looks as substantial as it must have looked when it was first constructed and set in position beneath its heavily tiled roof gables that make it look almost top-heavy.

You should not expect to find at Stokesay quite such a lavish display of period furniture and distinguished portraits as you will have seen elsewhere ; but you will certainly find a wealth of interesting detail in the chambers contained within these massive walls : a medieval stone fireplace with overmantel carved in oak in the Solar ; odd fragments of medieval carving here and there in the gatehouse and elsewhere ; and a fine timbered roof in the hall, well worth detailed inspection. Though not built on the grand scale, Stokesay is certainly one of England's more romantic places.

Shropshire

Weston Park

On A5, just west of Weston-under-Lizard, twelve miles north of Wolverhampton

Open at Easter; then on Wednesdays, Thursdays, Saturdays and Sundays throughout the five summer months

The entrance gates to this beautiful mansion are to be found at the junction of the main road and a minor road leading to the village of Tong and the main A41 Wolverhampton road. A long drive runs through open parkland, to swing left and lead directly to the house. The parkland that so beautifully surrounds the hall is yet another example of the genius of 'Capability' Brown. This is not one of the oldest of England's great houses, for its main front dates back only some three centuries; but it rightly claims to be one of the finest examples of building in the Restoration period. Indeed, restoration in its more usual sense is here the apt word, for successive generations of the owners have busied themselves redesigning and remodelling various aspects of the house. Much of the interior was remodelled in the eighteenth and nineteenth centuries,

and even today, in this mid-twentieth century, schemes are afoot for opening up yet more of the interior for the visitor's delectation.

The house is a treasury of fine pictures — by artists such as Holbein, Gainsborough, Van Dyck, Hoppner, to mention a few only; of fine furniture and rare and beautiful *objets d'art;* and here they find an incomparable setting. There is simplicity and dignity, for instance, in the great sweep of the marble and wrought-iron-balustraded staircase swinging upwards from the appropriately named Marble Hall to the upper floor. One of the loveliest of all the rooms is undoubtedly that named the Tapestry Room, with its priceless specimens from the Gobelin factory and furniture rich in Aubusson coverings. Hardly less impressive is the drawing room, spaciously conceived, with a ceiling supported by finely fluted columns.

The library, as is so often the case, combines a sense of age and tradition with an impression of being in regular use. The shelves laden with opulently bound volumes are looked down upon by portraits of the family, five of these being the work of Romney and Reynolds. Visitors with a particular interest in furniture will find much to delight and excite them here : not least the rare and beautiful sets of chairs by Hepplewhite and other great craftsmen of various periods and divers countries. Yet it need not be felt that Weston Park is just a museum, for house and contents are so well matched that each lends distinction to the other.

Somerset

Cothay Manor

Off A38, four miles west of Wellington

Open on Wednesdays from June to mid-September, and on the first Sunday of each summer month, also Wednesdays in August

This exquisite manor house has been fittingly and deservedly referred to as an 'architectural sleeping beauty.' It is located so far off the beaten track that you are entitled to feel a prince indeed if you have the patience to find your way to it. Leave the Taunton to Exeter main road, then, four miles south-west of Wellington, take a lane on the north side that is signposted to Greenham. The manor's own signposts do not appear for some time, but do not give up, for the object of your search will more than justify your perseverance. A sudden right-handed turn in the lane marks the point at which you should fork left into the short drive leading you straight to the mid-fifteenth-century gatehouse overlooking a charming ornamental water that was formed by damming a small tributary of the river Tone which idles by the western corner of the estate. The buildings are of the local pale rose-red sandstone, pleasantly contrasted with the paler stone from the Ham Hill quarries.

You pass through the gatehouse and arrive in a courtyard enclosed by the high walls of the manor house; originally it was cobbled but now well-cut turf emphasizes the beauty of the containing-walls. The chapel, a little room strangely moving in its simplicity and hint of age, is to be found close to the gateway. Most of Cothay is on the small scale — and the more enchanting for that, for there is an element of perfection in such building that is not always to be found in the more grandiose. Even the Great Hall is not so great as the term implies, but it is exquisite in its proportions and style, with a glorious roof and a Minstrels' Gallery which still gives access, as it originally did, to the bedrooms.

The Winter Parlour, the Gold Room (with its memorable fresco and other wall paintings), the oratory, the library, which was formerly the Undercroft, and the Solar, designed as the living-room for the women of the manor, are all beautiful in their several ways. Probably this last is most memorable, for the impression it gives of having been lived in and loved by generations of women. You leave Cothay with a memory of a warm and gracious stone-built manor house that has been the home of three West Country families spread over four centuries, and is lived in still.

Siskiyou County Library

Today's Date: Mon 08/03/15 03:09 PM

The California native landscape :
32871003864200
Date Due: **08/24/2015**

The map of the sky :
32871003687106
Date Due: **08/24/2015**

A guide to English country houses /
32871000259362
Date Due: **08/24/2015**

Total = 3 items checked out. Thank You!

Somerset

Montacute House

On A3088, four miles west of Yeovil

Open daily, except non-Bank Holiday Mondays and Tuesdays from March to October

This enormous mansion takes its name from the *mons acutus,* the steep-sided hill, on which it was built. Its foundations were laid in the year of the Armada, and the whole vast enterprise was completed, astonishingly in view of its size and the demand of its site, within little more than a decade, H-shaped, it is a magnificent specimen of Elizabethan building, its design enhanced, of course, by the golden glory of the Ham Hill stone of which it is so largely built. And it was designed and built on the heroic scale: it possesses both an east front and a west front of almost equal splendour and presence, instead of one being subordinated to the other; the rich and powerful nobility and gentry of the Tudor period built to impress, and great houses such as Montacute were 'status symbols' *par excellence* before the term had reached the somewhat debased, or at any rate contemptuous, connotation it possesses today.

One feature that will swiftly impress you is its element of symmetry; this is in strong contrast with the characteristics of medieval buildings (which you may or may not prefer). Montacute rises to three storeys, a veritable escarpment in golden stone, lit — as was the fashion of the period — with magnificently large and perfectly proportioned windows. The overall and dominant impression on the visitor is one of lofty dignity, subdued warmth of tone, and wide-eyed splendour.

The interior, of course, matches the exterior in splendour and exceeds it in detail. In the Great Hall look especially at the plasterwork in relief form which tells two stories in pictorial fashion. If you know the novels of Thomas Hardy (and here you are not far from the heart of his Wessex) you may be able to identify and interpret what you see. You proceed from one memorable room to another: to the library, or Great Chamber, to the sixty-yard-long Long Gallery, running the whole length of the mansion; to the Crimson Room, with its fine wainscotting, Lord Curzon's Room, the Hall Chamber and the Ante-Room, with its Raeburn portraits; a maze of rooms, each with its individual treasures — tapestries, panelling, heraldic glass, furniture. Indeed, knowing that Lord Curzon, sometime Viceroy of India, lived and died here, you gain some idea of how an English grandee lived in the heyday of his retirement.

Staffordshire

Blithfield Hall

On B5013 Rugeley-Abbots Bromley road, four miles north of Rugeley

Open on Wednesdays, Thursdays, Saturdays and Sundays from Easter to 5 October

As you approach this house from the direction of Abbots Bromley you notice a number of sheets of water : you might indeed term this a watery landscape. And as you leave the minor road that has wound its way among these sheets of water you at once begin to climb gently by way of a stretch of parkland overlooking the water to the house itself. It is a house that is some five hundred years old, and has been in the possession of one family for almost the whole of that time. Generation after generation of Bagots have devoted time and money and imagination and skill to making this home of theirs as they would wish it to be both for themselves and for their immediate descendants. It can be said here, more truly than is usually the case, that the house has 'grown up' with its occupants, being altered here, enlarged there, adapted, restored, renovated and even on occasion reduced, at the instigation of one generation or another. For all this, it has beautifully maintained and preserved its integrity. To pass through its gateway into the courtyard is to be swiftly conveyed into the heart of a well integrated and certainly well loved family home.

It possesses, of course, its splendid features : the noble oak Great Staircase — its treads and balusters carved from oak trees grown on the estate ; the Great Dining Room, with its magnificent barrel ceiling and its green and gold Elizabethan panelling ; the drawing room — L-shaped, most unusually for that period ; and other impressive rooms besides. But it contains one most unusual feature, perhaps unique, a feature that will delight children even more than adults : the Toy Museum. Here young visitors (and their parents too, of course) can take delight in

examining the toys and child's possessions of an older day : dolls'-house furniture, children's carriages, the exquisitely-wrought child's tea-services, the toy barrel-organs, Punch and Judy models, coaches and carts and much else, including treasures from abroad.

There are, too, whole rooms to be explored, including the Pink, the Yellow and the Blue Nurseries. It is these rooms, perhaps more than any other, that revive nostalgia in the elderly and wonder in the young. Here, then is a great house with something most unusual, most rewarding, to offer. It should on no account be missed.

Staffordshire

Wightwick Manor

Off A454 Wolverhampton-Bridgnorth road, three miles west of Wolverhampton

Open on Thursdays and Saturdays and Bank Holidays throughout the year; also on Wednesdays throughout the months of summer

This most unusual manor house gives the impression that it simply does not wish to be visited. You might drive past in either direction half a dozen times and within a hundred yards or so of it, and still not find it, unless you were very much on the alert. In fact, having taken the Bridgnorth road westwards out of Wolverhampton you should begin, after two miles or so, to look out for the Mermaid Inn which stands on your right-hand side. Just short of it, close alongside, is a narrow lane that climbs steeply between close-set banks of trees. Fifty or sixty yards up the lane, on your left-hand side, there is a gateway : you have, perhaps unexpectedly, arrived.

This place is a 'new boy' among the great houses of England, for it was built no more than eighty-odd years ago. You might be tempted to challenge the statement, for the style of building is that of the heavy half-timbering you may have become accustomed to in Cheshire, on the Welsh Border and elsewhere in what used to be good oak-growing country. In fact, it was deliberately built in this style by its first owner, and he was responsible for ensuring that the craftsmanship explicit in the timber and plasterwork, both in the exterior and the interior, should be the finest the eighties of the last century could produce. Wightwick Manor is essentially associated with the Pre-Raphaelite Movement ; indeed, it is something of a mecca for those to whom the term, today, is something other than one of abuse.

The ghost — or perhaps the word aura is more apt — of that fine artist-craftsman William Morris imbues the whole structure, quite apart from the fact that the rooms contain a most impressive collection of the Master's wallpapers and tapestries, together with tiles, both of his own work and that of his close associates and disciples. Inevitably the interior must strike you as dark, even gloomy, for the windows admit hardly sufficient light to combat the darkness of the oak timbers and panelling and the wall-hangings ; but somehow this is in keeping with the mood that the house induces, and you will find it hard to believe, as you pass from room to lovely room, over polished floors, that the building is less than a century old.

Suffolk

Ickworth

**On A143, three miles south-west of
Bury St Edmunds**

**Open on Wednesdays, Thursdays,
Saturdays, Sundays and Bank Holidays
from Easter to 5 October**

You will come upon this most unusual example of a great house immediately you enter the village of Horringer. A drive of only moderate length, branching off the road through the village, leads you to it ; but in fact only a photograph taken from the air could give you a real understanding of its layout, for it is most unusual in its overall design. In shape it is — perhaps uniquely among our great houses — not even circular but elliptical : a centrally placed rotunda contains a drawing room, a dining room, a library and a hall ; and from this central block two boldly curving corridors, which themselves incorporate the smoking room and the so-called Pompeian Room, lead at length to the east and the west wings. The house was designed almost as a challenge to convention and current thought by that most remarkable millionaire-cleric-globe-trotter, Bishop of Derry and Earl of Bristol, after whom the chief hotels in many a continental town and city are named. The place is not yet two centuries old, and in fact was never seen by its eccentric promoter, who died in Italy before this extravaganza in stone (as some would refer to it) was near completion. *c op./*

The Bishop-Earl was an inveterate collector of antiques and *objets d'art* and it would seem that a fair proportion of what he so assiduously collected is now housed within this strangely devised building. Here you will find marble statuary by such sculptors as Flaxman and Bouchardon ; portraits and other paintings by such artists as Kauffman, Hoppner, Lawrence, Zoffany, Eves and Cope ; Wilton carpets designed and woven for the rooms in which they have been laid. You will see a collection of family silver that can claim to be one of the most notable in the country ; and you can see, too, a wide and impressive variety of furniture, and smaller articles such as snuff-boxes, watches, majolica plates from Urbino, Sèvres vases, a Chinese (Ch'ien Lung) *famille rose* dinner-service, Meissen porcelain, and much more besides.

Ickworth does not impress you as having been lived in and loved ; it is rather a vast display-cabinet for a remarkable assemblage of valuables of classic rather than intimate quality. But you will have to agree that the objects are splendidly housed, and the house is surrounded by Lebanon and Indian cedars and Monterey cypresses that impart to it just a hint at any rate of informality, if not of intimacy.

Suffolk

Melford Hall

At junction of A134 Bury St Edmunds-Sudbury road and A1092 Clare-Long Melford road

Open on Wednesdays, Thursdays, Sundays and Bank Holidays from Easter to the end of September

The entrance gates to this fine house are to be found alongside the main road on the outskirts of one of the most beautiful villages in a county rich in such villages, Long Melford. Beside the entrance stands an attractive octagonal garden house, which gives a hint of the mellow beauty you find awaiting you when you have passed through the gateway and into the grounds. The gravel drive leads you, with one right-handed turn, straight to the E-shaped Elizabethan mansion whose fine red-brick wings seem to reach out towards you and enfold you as you approach.

Though some portions of the fabric may well be pre-Elizabethan, the main structure was built in the mid-sixteenth century by Sir William Cordell, Master of the Rolls to Elizabeth I. From the wings an array of six finely proportioned octagonal turrets reach up into the wide Suffolk sky, intermingled with stacks of elegantly shaped chimneys which, by contrast, perhaps seem more slender and insubstantial than they really are. This is a roof-scape of a particularly impressive character.

What will you find inside of special interest and attractiveness ? There is the great Banqueting Hall, two storeys in height and with an enormous fireplace ; the Regency Library has a notable display of shelving of oak, burr walnut and inlaid bands of ebony, revealing fine craftsmanship in a variety of beautifully grained timber. In the Hyde Parker Room there are outstanding portraits of the Earls and Baronets and their ladies by artists such as Reynolds, Northcote and Kneller. Perhaps the most restful room of all is the Blue Drawing Room, formerly the main dining room, with its mid-Georgian decor and the blue-and-white colour scheme that gives it its name.

Once the hall was moated ; today only a small section of the moat survives, between the great brick outer wall and the road beyond the gateway. In the gardens there is a charming example of Tudor domestic architecture, a gabled octagonal pavilion. The old, and essential, fish-ponds survive too : a reminder of the enforced self-sufficiency of these great houses in olden times. They add a nice domestic, almost nostalgic, touch. And just beyond the gates is the spacious village green, a reminder of the life that went on all about the great house and continues today.

Surrey

Clandon Park

On A246, three miles east of Guildford

Open on Mondays, Wednesdays, Saturdays and Sundays from mid-summer to the end of September

Two hundred and fifty years ago a Jacobean mansion was demolished on this site to make room for the present one, so that it is among the younger of our great houses. It does, however, rank as an outstanding as well as an early example of the Palladian style in English architecture, being the work of the Italian, Leoni. Not surprisingly it is virtually unaltered today, but it differs from the majority of mansions built in this period and style in that brick has been used instead of the customary stone. It thus possesses a warmth that has an immediate appeal for the visitor.

But it is the interior that will undoubtedly leave the strongest and most enduring impression, for here you will find a rewarding splendour of contents ideally housed and displayed. Look especially at the Palladio Room, with its most beautifully composed ceiling of stucco work. Examine the 'flock' wallpaper that dates from the latter part of the century in which the house was built : you may have seen its counterpart in the Victoria & Albert Museum ; the fine specimens of Louis XV furniture look especially well against such a background. And do not miss the State Bedroom, formerly known as the Green Drawing Room, with its very remarkable chimney-piece, and the State Bed, which is earlier by a good deal than the house itself.

It is probably true to say that the chief glories of Clandon Park are to be found in its ceilings : they rivet the attention and fire the imagination, not only in the room already mentioned but in the Red Drawing Room, the saloon, and the hall. By our standards of today, of course, they are overly ornate ; but they conform to a tradition maintained and executed by the master-craftsmen in plasterwork in almost every part of the country and on the Continent. The connoisseur of such features will derive pleasure from comparing and contrasting those he finds in the different great houses, every one of which has its own particular quality and distinction. And one most unusual feature that should on no account be overlooked is the Maori *whare*, or native hut, unexpectedly situated in an English garden, and evidence of the interest in New Zealand felt by one of the nineteenth-century owner-occupiers of Clandon.

Surrey

Polesden Lacey

On a minor road three miles north-west of Dorking

Open on Saturdays, Sundays and Bank Holiday Mondays, from March until mid-December. Also Tuesdays from May to August

Only a century and a half has flowed over this house with its melodious name. It was built as recently as 1824, to the designs of a man who was responsible for many beautiful buildings in Regency London. It is dignified rather than pretentious and few mansions can have been more exquisitely sited than this one, on a gentle slope that dips southwards to the valley below and seems thereby to enhance its air of poise and distinction. Without question, its most satisfying aspect is the long south front, overlooking the spacious parkland in which it is set, and distinguished by its fine colonnade of Ionic pillars. The exterior so handsomely displayed is virtually unaltered : this is how it was designed and built a hundred and fifty years ago.

The interior, however, is a different matter altogether. You enter it to find a characteristic example of the sort of setting an Edwardian hostess, accustomed to mixing with high society, would devise for herself and her entourage. The pervading atmosphere is that of gentility, dignity, serenity, poise : indeed, there is something essentially feminine about this interior, which offers the strongest possible contrast to the essentially masculine feel of some of the older great houses, particularly those which were originally fortified homes, or designed as castles.

The drawing room, above all, emphasizes this, with its gilded panelling and ceiling, which once graced an Italian palace, and its most beautiful Louis XV and XVI furniture, the Dresden and Chelsea china and the exquisitely delicate Chinese porcelain. There is more of this in the fine library, and also some superlative specimens of

Chippendale, as well as Queen Anne winged armchairs and furniture of Italian and Flemish origin two centuries older than the house. But for many visitors it may well be the Tea Room that leaves the strongest impression, with its exquisite needlework, its Louis XV furniture and the wholly charming Japanese 'insect cage' given to the owner of the house by the late Queen Mary. The treasures displayed at Polesden Lacey may be on a less sumptuous scale than those at some of the older great houses, but they are most effectively presented and blend perfectly with their gracious setting.

Sussex

Arundel Castle

Entered from the east outskirts of Arundel

Open on Mondays to Thursdays from mid-April to mid-June; on Fridays also until the end of September; and on Saturdays also during August

This imposing edifice dominating the little township was built some nine centuries ago to serve as the prime feudal stronghold on the Sussex coast; it is now the country seat of the Duke of Norfolk. Though a good deal of the original structure was destroyed in the middle of the seventeenth century, to be subsequently rebuilt by a succession of owners, certain portions of it still remain practically as they were when the masons laid down their tools soon after the Norman Conquest. The drawbridge and barbican and keep date back to that period, and one of the glories of the castle is the Norman arch over the inner gateway, which has survived nine long centuries. If you look carefully you can still see marks of the cannon balls that wrought such destruction three centuries ago, notably on the walls of the barbican tower.

It is not surprising that so much of the castle should have survived a series of sieges — two during the first half of the twelfth century and the third when the Roundheads took the castle virtually intact during the Civil War — for some of the walls, of flint and local Pulborough stone as well as stone from Caen in Normandy, are no less than ten feet thick. Indeed, it is the exterior that will make the strongest impact upon the visitor. For here you will find all that you would expect from a castle as ancient as Arundel : keep and barbican, towers and curtain-walls, battlements and tilting-grounds, dungeons and vaults, drawbridge and inner bailey. History has been enacted here, and even amid a crowd of sightseers it is not hard to imagine that you are rubbing shoulders with the Norman, Roger Montgomery, with the Empress Matilda who,

eight centuries ago, slept in the chamber above the Norman archway, or with the legendary Bevis of Hampton who, as Warden of the Castle in remote times, hurled his sword, Mongley, from the battlements into the spacious parkland and ordained that he should be buried at the spot where it fell. Mongley may be seen on one of the great pillars in the armoury — a fitting resting-place for such a sword.

The Barons' Hall, Picture Gallery, private chapel, drawing room, dining room and other rooms all contain their respective treasures, fascinating in their detail ; but the dominant impression that will remain is the exterior : grey monumental stone set in an ample frame of green turf and splendid stands of beech and oak.

Sussex

Bateman's

One mile south of Burwash

Open from 1 March until 31 October, except on Fridays

Bateman's Lane branches south off the main A265 Hawkhurst to Lewes road, right in the village of Burwash. It drops, at first steeply, then more gently, to flatten out in the wide and shallow valley of the River Dudwell. In the heart of this charming valley, sequestered behind its tall yew hedges, lies this three-hundred-years-old house of stone. Rudyard Kipling lived within its grey walls for some thirty years until his death in 1936. This was the setting he appropriately chose for two of his best-loved books, 'Rewards and Fairies' and 'Puck of Pook's Hill'. The view to Pook's Hill is shown on the map, to the south-west of the house itself.

In the early seventeenth century this part of Sussex — though it is difficult to believe it as you survey the rural scene today — was iron-founding country. Bateman's was built almost exactly three hundred years before Kipling's death by the owner of Nether Forge, which was on the bank of the Dudwell a quarter of a mile away ; he was one of the great iron-masters of his day, and the house he planned has something of the massiveness and grim dignity you might expect from a man in his trade. It is, in addition, a notable example of the country style of architecture of the Jacobean period, built mainly of local stone and topped by a beautifully proportioned central stack of chimneys, not in the same stone but built of brick. It is evident that the mason primarily responsible for the fabric was a first-rate craftsman, even something of an artist, for you are unlikely to find more pleasingly designed mullions and dripstone mouldings than these even in the most pretentious great houses.

The interior of Bateman's has hardly been changed in the thirty-odd years since Kipling's wife died. Because the mullioned windows are small and much of the interior is heavily panelled, the immediate impression is that the rooms are dark. Yet you will at once sense that a keen literary life was lived here, amid an abundance of books and other treasures on display in the hall, the drawing room and the study. But look out through the windows and you catch the glint of the stream flowing across the grounds, a glimpse of oasts, the pear walk, the wishing-well and tree-shadowed, sunlit lawns framed within the slopes of the valley Rudyard Kipling loved so well.

Sussex

Glynde Place

In Glynde village, four miles south-east of Lewes

Open on Spring and August Bank Holidays, and on Thursdays, Saturdays and Sundays from May to end of December

Glynde village lies just about one mile to the north of A27, the road linking Lewes with the coast at Pevensey Bay, and is approached by an ascending lane that branches off the main road two miles or so south-east of Lewes, and cleaves its way through banks of trees, to open out in the heart of the village. Here is an assembly of small cottages of local flint and mellow brickwork, some of them eighteenth-century, some of them a good deal earlier. They nestle here on the lower slope of the Downs which drop southwards and shelter them from winds from the north.

The entrance to this house is by a short drive at the upper end of the village. It leads you directly to a most beautiful archway of warm brick and cold flint ; through it, before you swing round to the main doors of the house, you catch a breathtakingly beautiful vista of rolling and terraced parkland studded with shapely stands of trees, falling away eastwards and southwards to the horizon. The house itself is built of stone from Caen and of flints from the local flint-and-chalk beds of the Downs, and dates back to Tudor times. Actually, there has been a succession of buildings on this site, probably from Roman times twelve centuries earlier still.

No small part of Glynde's charm lies in the fact that it was built round a central quadrangle, reminiscent of an Oxford or Cambridge college. This emphasizes the seclusion, the timelessness, of the place ; it is flanked by velvet lawns, and on one of these there grows a rose bush known to have been planted more than a century ago. It has most evidently been a home for many generations, and is a home today ; it gives an immediate impression of having been truly lived in and cherished. It is filled, though not unduly crowded, with paintings and bronzes and fine panelling ; the spacious and well-lit gallery is especially noteworthy for this. The Great Staircase deserves a close look, as do the chimney-pieces in gallery and hall, the work of a local craftsman that can stand comparison with corresponding pieces by designers whose work, in more grandiose settings, has achieved a greater reputation. Indeed, it would be hard to find a more satisfying example of domestic architecture, conceived in the reign of Elizabeth I, to delight the eye in the reign of Elizabeth II.

Sussex

Great Dixter

In Northiam, off A28 Ashford-Hastings road

Open at Easter; then daily from the end of April until 28 September, except on Mondays

A narrow lane that branches west out of the heart of the village leads directly to this most beautiful example of fifteenth-century half-timbered manor house architecture. A notice at the gate warns visitors that the flagstones leading to the porch are uneven and can be treacherous, especially if they are wet. The warning is timely, for your eye will certainly have been caught and held by the timberwork of that heavy gabled porch with its diamond-lead-paned window matching that in the great gable to the right as you face it. This impressive timberwork is constructed of good Sussex oak; but the timbers have been there for five long centuries, and in that time have bent and twisted beneath their load; today there is hardly a horizontal or true vertical to be seen. The very lopsidedness of the façade is an added attraction.

Within, the main attraction is the huge timbered Great Hall, forty feet long by twenty-five feet wide and over thirty feet in height, one of the largest surviving timber-built halls in the country. It is indeed constructed on the heroic scale: the main tie-beam spanning its entire width was hewn from a single oak tree, its curved bracing beams from another; and, more unusual still, since this is timber-, not stone-built, is the fact that the hall contains massive hammer-beams. Such restoration as has proved inescapable over the centuries has been most skilfully and unobtrusively executed, much of it by Edwin Lutyens, architect of New Delhi, whose wise and understanding touch was well suited for such an operation. Great Dixter is completely integrated; and, as might be expected, the antique furniture which is so rich an integral part blends quite perfectly with its setting.

The house finds a perfect setting in its gardens, which have been developed only during the last half-century of occupation by the present owners, with the co-operation of Lutyens, who wisely recommended that the extensive outbuildings should be made an integral part of the whole. For many visitors these gardens, and the flowers and shrubs and small trees they contain, including some fine topiary work, will be the chief attraction; but you can never be unconscious of the brooding presence of the half-timbered edifice which dominates them so unobtrusively yet so decisively.

Sussex

Parham

Off A283, four miles south of Pul-borough

Open from Easter to 5 October on Sundays, Wednesdays, Thursdays and Bank Holidays

Though the Downs rise not far away, this beautiful sixteenth-century mansion is set in the heart of a spacious and level-lying deer park which affords the visitor ample time to take in its dignity and serenity as he approaches it by way of its long, curving drive. What presents itself to view is a spaciously windowed façade ; behind this is to be found a complex of buildings, portions of which may well incorporate the remains of a much earlier building erected on the site when it belonged to the Abbot of Westminster. Tall and harmoniously proportioned chimney-stacks rise above the level roof-ridge into the clear Sussex sky ; great gable is matched by great gable, lesser gable with lesser gable ; but in all of them the fine mullioned windows are more than ordinarily spacious, and lend an air of lightness and openness to a structure massive enough in its weight of stonework to hint at secrets well hidden.

As with many great houses of this sort of age, there have been additions and alterations as the centuries idled by. But it is unlikely that you will be conscious of this at Parham, unless you have read its story in some detail and look at it with an appraising eye, for the alterations have been skilfully and unobtrusively carried out, by experts commissioned by a succession of owners who have loved their home and been determined that it should not be in any way marred by clumsy treatment.

Outstanding among Parham's many fine rooms is the Long Gallery, which runs the full length of the south front and is almost a hundred and sixty feet in length. In this room – and surely 'room', here, is a misnomer ? – there are many objects of unusual interest. You will find an embroidered saddle that was actually used by James II ; even rarer as an object, there is an adjustable chair more than three hundred years old. But you will soon realize that every room contains its own rare and interesting exhibits, and you will need plenty of time to make your way among them if you are to savour them to the full. Spare a moment, however, now and then, to look out through those great windows at the deer park, the ornamental water, and, beyond, the lovely Sussex landscape spreading outwards to the distant horizon.

Sussex

Petworth House

Entrance on the north-east side of Petworth

Open on Wednesdays, Thursdays, Saturdays and Bank Holidays from April to October

The village, or township, of Petworth lies at the junction of the A272 Haywards Heath to Winchester and A283 Guildford to Petworth roads : a narrow, twisting road passes through it, and you should halt at the very edge of the village to find the gateway.

The house originally built on this site belonged to a famous family — one might rather say 'dynasty' — that of the Northumberland Percies, whose northern fortress, Alnwick Castle, lies four hundred miles to the north of this peaceful Sussex countryside. It was owned by the Percies for some twenty generations. But now only the thirteenth-century chapel remains from that remote period, for the original edifice was torn down and a new one built in its place some three centuries ago ; and there have been further alterations and additions in subsequent years. Probably the most notable external feature is the enormously long main façade, the famous west front, which is over a hundred yards in length. Behind it are to be found the famous state rooms ; among these is the great Carved Room, which claims to be the finest achievement of that master-carver, Grinling Gibbons, and one of the most outstanding state rooms anywhere in the country, royal palaces included.

The splendour of the edifice is matched by the splendour and variety of its contents. You will see displayed on the walls of the Staircase Hall, the Somerset Room, the so-called Beauty Room, the Turner Room, the Marble Hall and the Grinling Gibbons Room (to mention six only of the many great rooms at Petworth) paintings by Hobbema and Reynolds, Kneller, Teniers, Millet, Lely and Van Dyck, Clint, Zoffany, Franz Hals, Holbein and Turner, amid scores of others by artists hardly less well-known. You will find sculpture, panelling, clocks, Kang Hsi Mandarin jars, vellum manuscripts, Louis XVI furniture, Roman statuary and Venetian chairs, Meissen and Chelsea porcelain, needlework (including some attributed to Lady Jane Grey) : all this, and much else, justifies the claim of Petworth House to possess one of the most varied and valuable private art collections in the country. And the house and parkland are surrounded by a perimeter wall no less than fourteen miles in circumference : the length of the wall built by the Turks to protect their city of Constantinople !

129

Warwickshire

Charlecote Park

Just west of A429 Warwick-Moreton-in-the-Marsh road, six miles south of Warwick

Open daily, except non-Bank Holiday Mondays, from April to September

There was a house here eight centuries ago; it was replaced by descendants of the original builders four centuries ago, and the mellow brick-and-stone detached gatehouse that is its chief glory today is their handiwork, though the greater part of the immense edifice is of later date than Elizabethan, having been added to during the centuries since the gatehouse was built to give access to the courtyard within. The approach to it is through a deer park with stands of magnificent trees; traditionally, it was here that the youthful Shakespeare was arrested for poaching.

Because so much of the remodelling of the house was carried out during the first half of the last century you will probably be impressed by the fact that within its walls you are surrounded at the same time by the antique and by the Victorian; yet the two periods blend uncannily well, for all the difference in years that lie between them. The original Minstrels' Gallery has gone from the Great Hall, but there is still the fine timbered roof; and as you look up at this you are standing on a marble floor which came from Venice. There are Tudor rarities in the dining room, and some exceptionally fine specimens of furniture and tapestry in the library. There are more tapestries in the appropriately named Tapestry Room, notably two panels of Flemish work portraying scenes said to be based on the Battle of Edgehill, in which the Lucy family of Charlecote fought on the King's side. Even more beautiful, perhaps, are the hangings of satin damask which adorn the walls of the drawing room and are of Chinese origin. Here too you will find curtains of crimson silk and a superb specimen of Axminster carpet which goes well with wall-hangings and curtains alike.

Not the least interesting feature of the place, and an unusual one, is the old Brew House on the south side of the forecourt: a reminder of the self-sufficiency of these old-established country seats, where beer was brewed in great quantities for the large community of servants and others living in and about them. Near the Brew House is the Coach House, with its array of vehicles owned by the gentry who occupied Charlecote down the years: another relatively intimate touch in a house which, today, is rather more of a museum than a house that is lived in.

Warwickshire

Compton Wynyates

On a minor road five miles east of Shipston-on-Stour and eight miles west of Banbury

Open at Easter; then on Wednesdays, Saturdays and Bank Holidays until September; and also on Sundays from June to August

You descend a narrow, tree-shaded lane from the main road, and should do this with care, for otherwise you might drive right past this most outstandingly beautiful house without descrying it. Unlike so many others, approached by a mounting or at least level drive, this lies near-hidden at the foot of a descending drive that winds among trees. It brings you to the mellow brick and stone porch with its dedication in Latin to 'My Lord, King Henry VIII'. This glorious building is the Warwickshire home of the Marquess of Northampton, and has been in the family's ownership for eight centuries, though the building you see today dates back no further than Tudor days. Henry VIII certainly stayed here on more than one occasion: one of the state bedrooms is appropriately named Henry VIII's Room, and its stained-glass window bears the emblem of the King, as well as those of Aragón, León and Castile – it is believed that Queen Katharine of Aragón was with him on one of his visits here.

This beautiful example of Tudor architecture at its finest lies sequestered in a hollow of the tree-grown hills, a pink jewel in a quite perfect setting. By no means its least inviting feature, on first approach from the slopes above the house, is its array of ornate chimneys. The moat which originally defended the house is there no more; but the gardens that lie about it are more than ordinarily beautiful, not least because on one side they spread almost level and on others rise gently beneath close-set trees to form a backcloth to the building seen first from the south-west approach. On the north-east side there is the famous display of ingenious topiary work: a feature much beloved by owners of such mansions down the years, and one that gives much pleasure to those of us who come from smaller homes and gardens to admire the resources of those who have been able to maintain the great tradition.

As for the historic treasures to be seen within, these are innumerable; nor is this surprising in view of the long and eventful centuries that have flowed over the roof and chimneys, the brick and stone walls and mullioned windows of this, perhaps the most beautifully designed of all the early Tudor mansions that constitute our heritage.

Warwickshire

Coughton Court

On A435 Birmingham-Cheltenham road, two miles north of Alcester

Open on Wednesdays, Thursdays, Saturdays, Sundays and Bank Holidays, from May to September; also less frequently during April and October

This lovely mansion stands on the edge of the Forest of Arden, in 'Shakespeare country'; it also stands on the edge of a busy main road. But it is fortunate in possessing a beautiful avenue of great elm trees, which help to screen it from the latter and to remind the visitor of the former. So, though it lies so close to the traffic streaming to and from one of our greatest industrial cities, it somehow contrives to seem quiet, undisturbed, turned in upon itself, a haven of serenity in a busy, unheeding outside world. Though now it is National Trust property, it has been the home of the ancient Throckmorton family for not far short of six hundred years.

Its most immediately noticeable feature as you swing up the drive towards it, parallel with the avenue of elms, is the magnificent central gatehouse, castellated and multi-turreted, formerly approached by a drawbridge spanning a moat, built in the earliest years of Henry VIII. The battlemented wings on either side are later than the gatehouse by more than two centuries, but have been so designed as to lend strength to the gatehouse they flank and to blend not unharmoniously with it, though so much later in date. It is through the gatehouse that you must pass to gain entrance to the beautiful courtyard and the alluring gardens that lie behind and beyond.

As to the interior, the hall itself, into which you immediately pass, is in fact the base of the gatehouse, and you should look out especially for the fan tracery of its fine ceiling. There is some beautiful timberwork in the interior, notably in the wings that fan out behind the gatehouse on either side; in every one of the rooms you will find some historic piece to hold the eye and set the imagination working. Here, for instance, is the Dole Gate of an ancient convent of which a Throckmorton was Abbess at the time of the Dissolution; here is a chair made out of wood taken from the bed in which Richard III slept on the night before Bosworth Field. And here – a morbid relic indeed – is Mary Queen of Scots' chemise, with a crimson stain on it reputed to be from the blood which flowed from her veins when she was beheaded at Fotheringay. This is indeed a repository of history; and the relics are the more memorable for the quietness and withdrawnness of their lovely setting.

Warwickshire

Packwood House

On B4439, two miles south-east of Hockley Heath on A34 Birmingham-Stratford-on-Avon road

Open on Tuesdays, Wednesdays, Thursdays, Saturdays and Bank Holiday Mondays throughout most of the year, though less often during the winter months

Though from the map this house appears to be quite simple to locate, almost on an important main road north to a great city, it is in fact elusive in the extreme, for it lies within a triangle formed by two very minor roads, neither of which seems likely to lead you anywhere at all. But keep your eyes open for the National Trust symbol at the junction of the two lanes, and you will find that it is within a few hundred yards. In any case do not give up your search, for if you do you will miss one of the most beautiful, and beautifully sited, of the smaller houses in the whole country.

Appropriately, it lies in what remains of the Forest of Arden : this is 'Shakespeare country' and his birthplace and that of his wife are not far away ; also the deer park in which as a youth he was apprehended by the gamekeepers. You are in timber country too,

and immediately you enter the house you will realize this, for the main structure is timber built, and it dates from the middle of the sixteenth century. The exterior of the house, however, is of brick and stone, having been added to at various periods, though always with such taste and discretion as to make the result homogeneous. The range of brick and stone buildings at right angles to the main façade date from a century later than the original fabric, but harmonize perfectly with it, as do the great walls and the gazebos that confront them across the turf.

For all the beauty and dignity of the interior – the Great Hall with its mullioned windows, the dining room with its seventeenth-century Flemish glass, the Inner Hall with its tapestries and the drawing room with its Charles II and Queen Anne furniture – it is more than possible that you will

remember most vividly the exterior. And not least the gracious gardens and the superb yew topiary work designed and planted three hundred years ago. These enormous yew trees have assembled about themselves the tradition of 'The Sermon on the Mount', 'The Apostles', 'The Evangelists' and 'The Master'. The pattern in which they were planted, and their various sizes and shapes, lend themselves to the tradition. Among them, you find yourself in a great temple of greenery, and instinctively drop your voice. Rarely can a great house have been given a more perfect setting than you will find here.

Warwickshire

Ragley Hall

On A435 Birmingham-Cheltenham road, two miles south-west of Alcester

Open at Easter, and on Tuesdays, Wednesdays, Thursdays, Saturdays, Sundays and Bank Holiday Mondays until the end of September

A mile-long drive serpentines through undulating parkland containing splendid oak trees, climbing gently into a belt of close-set giants that open to reveal suddenly the great house facing you, its forecourt and wrought-iron balustrated steps alive with peacocks : you could hardly hope for a happier first sight of a spaciously windowed façade. Here is a mansion that has been the home of one family, the country seat of the Marquess of Hertford, since it was built almost exactly three hundred years ago. It is a home that has been consistently lived in down the years ; the present generation of owners has followed the example of earlier occupants in altering it in detail here and there in such a fashion that their house is essentially alive as well as the embodiment of a sustained tradition. The great portico, for instance, was added to the main structure just a century after the hall was built ; the present owner states emphatically that it is his constant aim not merely to maintain the place but 'to make it even more beautiful than it is now'.

There will be no question in most visitors' minds that in the present instance the interior is more memorable even than the exterior, beautiful as that is. The magnificent Great Hall, with its superb ceiling medallion, is perhaps the show-piece of the whole place but many may be inclined to feel that the library, with its many thousands of handsomely bound and housed volumes, is even more to their taste. It is said to be the Marquess's favourite room ; and small wonder, for it is at once impressive and – if such a word can be used here – cosy.

The two dining rooms, the Blue Drawing Room, the Red Saloon, the Prince Regent's Bedroom, with its massive and curiously proportioned four-poster bed and somewhat coldly forbidding oval portrait of Queen Victoria, the South Staircase Hall (there are no fewer than seven staircases at Ragley Hall), and the Green Drawing Room have each their specific treasures in pictures, furniture, silverware, porcelain, china and glassware, on which the roving eye may feast and take delight. Not the least attractive feature of this place is the frequent change in the contents of some of the rooms, so that with each successive visit you seem to find something that you had not seen before. This policy of deliberate change is unusual, and rewarding.

Westmorland

Levens Hall

On A6, five miles south of Kendal

Open daily, except Fridays and Satur-days, from 1 May until mid-September

If you are travelling north, towards the Lake District, you turn abruptly off the dual carriageway section of this main road just short of the beautiful Levens Bridge spanning the river Kent. A short drive, and a swing to the left, and you are facing a pele-tower more than six centuries old which has been most skilfully and successfully incorporated by a subsequent owner, in more peaceful days, into a fine block of stone buildings, well-windowed and gabled, that may be entered by a short, steep flight of steps. This is essentially an Elizabethan structure (apart from the much older pele-tower), most of it dating from a year or two before the defeat of the Spanish Armada. Even the exterior gives a hint that this house is one that is lived in, and not a mere repository of history; as soon as you pass through the doorway at the top of the steps this impression is emphatically reinforced. Here men and women down the centuries have lived life to the full ; and they have been fortunate in that they have been far removed from the Border Country strife that involved so many generations.

It is not at all easy to decide which individual room makes the most lasting impression, for all are integrated into a community of rooms, lived in and loved. There are portraits and pieces of furniture of great value and great antiquity ; there are, too, examples of craftsmanship — notably the harpsichords — for which the present owner is responsible as artist-craftsman ; there are coats of arms, there is silverware, exquisite ceiling plasterwork, and wallpapers — notably in the dining room and one small bedroom — made, in fact, of Cordova leather three hundred years old and so lovingly cared for

that it might have been placed on the walls only yesterday, except that it possesses a patina that could only have been acquired over many years.

Tradition here is strong : the tradition of an integrated family life. Legend, too, is strong : that of the Grey Lady, the Pink Lady, the Black Dog, the White Fawn. But as is fitting in so serene a house, there is gentleness, even humour, in these legends. Do not leave Levens Hall, however, without lingering in its famous topiary gardens, almost without peer in this country, the masterpiece of a man who planted yew and beech here two centuries and a half ago.

Wiltshire

Avebury Manor

On A361 Swindon-Devizes road, one mile north of its junction with A4 London-Bath main road

Open daily, except on Tuesdays in May, July and August; on Saturdays and Sundays in April, June and September; and also on Bank Holidays

This beautiful Elizabethan manor house has the unique distinction of standing practically at the heart of one of the most famous megalithic remains in the world – the Stone Circle of Avebury, reputedly the true heart of prehistoric England. On all sides of it rise the immense monoliths that were erected here some four thousand years ago and still stand as silent witnesses to the spiritual life of a community that has vanished from the face of the land, leaving only these impressive traces.

On this pagan site a monastery was built; and it was on this pagan-cum-monastic land that this sixteenth-century manor house was built: in its foundations and fabric there is clear evidence that material was taken from the twelfth-century building, probably a Benedictine establishment. So that you see here as it were a palimpsest of history and prehistory too: a richness of tradition hardly to be matched elsewhere. But, though it is so rich in historical and prehistoric record, it is also a home cherished by its owner. There is something a little disconcerting in the knowledge that from a setting so ancient, so steeped in prehistory, a distinguished scientist goes off regularly to research with equipment including electron microscopes.

His lovely home is full of rare possessions. In the Great Hall there is an adroit mixture of Italian, Spanish, Chinese and Elizabethan English objects: tables, mirrors, altar candlesticks, paintings; the hall, which was originally the Elizabethan Little Parlour, has early panelling and a rare Worcester dessert service and an iron chest from the first Elizabeth's day, among other rarities. Drawing Room, Crimson Room, Elizabethan Bedroom, State Bedroom, Chinese Landing and other named rooms all have their store of *objets d'art* portraying a period or a style or the work of some individual artist-craftsman. And the manor itself is surrounded by gardens and parkland in which will be found rare animals, including Four-horned and Soay sheep and Formosan deer: flowers, plants and shrubs, too, of course, and some topiary work. You enter by way of the Monk's Garden, turning your back for the time being on the prehistoric and entering the realm of recorded and living history.

Wiltshire

Longleat House

Off B3092, four and a half miles south-east of Frome

Open every day of the year, Sundays included, with the exception of Christmas Day

You can approach this house either by a minor road, B3092, which leads you to its main entrance, or by the A362 Frome–Warminster road and a subsequent toll-road; in either case the signposting is lavish and arresting. LION RESERVE, you read, on bold blue-and-white signs; for many visitors they are the main attraction.

Though the lions are comparative newcomers, this enormous mansion, appropriately dubbed 'the first great house of the English Renaissance', has been the home of the Marquess of Bath and his ancestors for four hundred years. His remote ancestor, from whose inspiration the house arose, died shortly before the coming of the Spanish Armada, and after watching the child of his imagination slowly grow from the ruins of an ancient priory into the glorious place it is today. With the exception of one or two additions midway through the centuries there has been little significant change.

There is an immense amount to see, and to remember. The Great Hall, with its magnificent hammer-beam roof, its armorial bearings and its fine hunting scenes; the State Dining Room; the saloon, which was formerly the traditional Long Gallery; and the drawing room: these are so rich in treasures that the eye is dazzled and the mind confused; a succession of visits, well spaced, seems the only solution. The furniture and Flemish tapestries and French porcelain, the sculptured mantelpieces and ceiling paintings and Italian embroidery, all this (and so much else) tends to overwhelm by its sheer variety of splendour. As is almost invariably the case in such mansions, the Grand Staircase, with the family State Chariot beneath its second flight of steps, is an object of beauty in its own right: functionalism subordinated to craftsmanship.

The spacious grounds are a fitting frame for the splendour and dignity of the house they encompass; lawns and lakes and Orangery, the parkland laid out by 'Capability' Brown (who would have shuddered at the thought of a Lion Reserve to be incorporated at some distant date!). Surfeited perhaps by what you have seen within the fabric of this centuries-old home, you may well decide to recuperate your flagging powers in the vast expanse of tree-shaded lawn and ornamental water of which you have from time to time caught inviting glimpses from Longleat's huge windows.

Wiltshire

Lydiard Mansion

**On a minor road just north of A420
Swindon-Chippenham road, four miles
west of Swindon**

**Open on Wednesdays, Thursdays,
Fridays, Saturdays and Sundays
throughout the year**

You must show some perseverance as well as imagination to arrive successfully at the entrance to this house. It seems to be almost perverse in its determination to resist being located. From the map, it does not even appear to be on a road at all, though it does not at first glance seem too remote from the main road — if only it could be reached from it. Moreover, in this part of the country, the Wiltshire-Dorset border, you are in a region of curious village names, at once alluring and puzzling. There is Lydiard Millicent, for example ; there is Cliffe Pypard ; there is Bradenstoke-cum-Clack. Resolutely you must put aside the temptation to see if these really exist, and instead make for Lydiard Tregoze. You may or may not ever find the village so charmingly named, but up a lane to your right (coming from the other Lydiard) there is a gateway almost hidden by trees ; it opens to a twisting drive, tree-embowered, that ends as it were at the back door among the outbuildings of the mansion, now maintained by the Corporation of nearby Swindon.

The estate in which it stands has been in the ownership of the St John family for more than five hundred years ; but though there was formerly a medieval house on the site, the house you now see is by no means as old as the family of the owners, nothing like so old as the references in Domesday Book would suggest. It was, in fact, largely rebuilt in the mid-eighteenth century. As you look at its south and east fronts you will appreciate that it presents the somewhat austere, some might say forbidding, exterior so often favoured in that period of building. But it contains many treasures still, even though all too many of the original ones were sold by the successors of the 3rd Viscount Bolingbroke in the early part of the nineteenth century, and subsequently. But connoisseurs of fine plasterwork will find here much to please them, and there is a simplicity, even an austerity, within that offers a nice contrast to the ornateness of some other great houses.

Probably the beautiful parkland and gardens will remain the most memorable feature of Lydiard : they are beautifully maintained, and the balance of smooth lawns, trim box hedges and severe classical lines produces a sense of deep satisfaction.

Wiltshire

Wilton House

In Wilton, at junction of A30 and A36 Salisbury roads

Open on Tuesdays to Saturdays inclusive from April to September, also on Bank Holidays

This is one of the truly great houses of England, the home for four hundred years of the Earls of Pembroke and the home today of the 16th Earl; it was a gift from Henry Tudor to his remotest ancestor and a long line of descendants has seen to it that this former priory was enriched, generation by generation, as it is still being enriched to this day. Both the interior and exterior of this Tudor mansion, as it was originally, have been rebuilt down the centuries (notably in the early stages at the hands of that master-craftsman Inigo Jones) so that to enter it now is to pass through the portals of one of the most spectacularly splendid of all our great houses.

Inigo Jones's great opportunity (of which he made the fullest possible use) came at the time of a disastrous fire in the mid-seventeenth century, and he was largely responsible for the magnificent sequence of state rooms immediately behind the imposing south front. Some impression of the extent of the mansion may be obtained simply from naming a few of its rooms: the Double-Cube Room, the Single-Cube Room (technical terms, these), the Hunting Room, the Colonnade Room, the Great Ante Room, the Corner Room, the Gothic Hall, the Large Smoking Room, the Upper Cloisters — Wilton's version of the traditional Long Gallery — and many more besides. This is more than a house, it is a mansion with many mansions contained within it; and all of them designed, decorated and furnished with taste and distinction. Indeed, there is a strong probability that you may be overwhelmed by the sheer magnificence of all that surrounds you. If this is the case, you must take temporary refuge in the superbly designed gardens, screening yourself from the riches, and the sheer opulence, beneath the widespread arms of the immense seventeenth-century cedars that are so dominant a feature of the place, and perhaps taking a covert glance the while across the greensward at the impressive Palladian bridge that spans the water beneath it with such massive and classical dignity.

But you will return, of course, for there is so much still to see. The Pembrokes have been enthusiastic yet discerning collectors down the years, and Wilton, their four-centuries-old home, is the repository of all they have found and made their own.

Yorkshire

Browsholme Hall

On a minor road from Whalley to Whitewell, six miles north-west of Clitheroe, fifteen miles north-east of Preston

Open on Thursdays, Saturdays, Sundays and Bank Holidays from Good Friday until mid-October

This house, of beautifully mellowed stone, was built four hundred and fifty-odd years ago on the site of a very much older house built of wattle-and-daub. It is very much less easy to find than many others, for it lies off a road so unassuming that you may be tempted to decide that it is not worth exploring. Here you are in country where Lancashire and the West Riding of Yorkshire make common ground ; here, not surprisingly the Wars of the Roses were a very real factor in men's lives. Immediately to the north of Browsholme the ground rises steeply to the ancient and forbidding stretch of border land known as the Trough of Bowland and the Forest of Bowland.

You are not conscious of this, however, as you approach the hall, for its mellow stone façade glows warmly and invitingly, and you will linger at the Jacobean entrance before entering the Tudor Hall (but you should remember to look back again once more as you depart, for the façade is worth more than a single glance). The Tudor Hall was originally the great communal 'eating room'; it had its two sections, 'above' and 'below' the salt, and occupied the main portion of the ground floor. From this you pass through room after room, each noteworthy for some treasure that makes it memorable. There is the drawing room, with its superb marble chimney-piece and mahogany doors; there is the Regency elegance of the dining room, in strong contrast to the old 'eating room', with its unique Chippendale sideboard; there is the Velvet Room, on the upper floor, once hung all with velvet and still containing a fine Elizabethan four-poster bed. You reach this floor by way of the Main Staircase and corridors, with their oak carving, their

Brussels and Flemish tapestries and their fine equestrian portraits: as so often, the staircase is memorable in its own right.

Browsholme Hall has been the home of the Parkers — official 'park-keepers' to the ancient game-preserves and deer-forest of Radholme since the Middle Ages — for centuries; it is their cherished home still. Successive generations have added to, carefully altered, restored and beautified, their home. By a happy touch, they have made much use of local talent among the Lancashire and Yorkshire craftsmen of the district, so that there is a tacit memorial to their skill at almost every turn.

Yorkshire

Burton Agnes Hall

On A166 Great Driffield-Bridlington road, midway between the two towns

Open daily, except Saturdays, from 1 May to mid-October

A short, steep, curving lane leaves the main road in the village and climbs directly to the grounds, dominated by the house high up above the surrounding countryside. It has been the home of one family for three and a half centuries, and remains their home; but the building itself, which dates back to the end of the sixteenth century and was in fact begun shortly after the defeat of the Spanish Armada, stands on a site formerly occupied by a small manor house built eight hundred years ago, parts of which can still be detected if you examine the fabric carefully enough.

You are likely to subscribe to the view held by many that Burton Agnes Hall is one of the loveliest of all the great Elizabethan houses. It is notable for the skilful and artistic blending of mellow red brick and fine stone quoins. You will notice this especially in the

152

great gatehouse, whether viewed from the hall itself or from the gardens, whose serene lawns are dotted about with a hundred beautifully shaped yews. For some the gatehouse may be the dominant memory: a rounded arch beneath massive brick and stonework, flanked by octagonal towers with lead-covered cupolas; on it you can read the date 1610, and note the arms of King James I.

The interior is no less memorable. Look especially for the great carving in alabaster depicting the story of the Wise and the Foolish Virgins, and the West Screen, as a whole in the Great Hall. Look out, too, for the chimney-piece in the drawing room, with its huge carving, in oak this time, of the symbolical figures depicting such ancient themes as The Dance of Death. In the Garden Gallery you may feast your eyes on the work of comparatively recent artists: men such as Cézanne, Renoir, Gauguin, Matisse and Augustus John. And, as usual in the larger Elizabethan houses, you will find the Great Staircase, a superb example of intricate design and craftsmanship and a rare specimen of the type of construction involving twin newel-posts.

Panelling, tapestries, chimney-pieces, paintings and sculpture abound on every hand. And for those with a taste for the macabre there is the tradition of the Queen's Bedroom, allegedly haunted by Anne Griffith, who declared that if her skull were not buried within the fabric she would haunt the place for ever.

Yorkshire

Castle Howard

Off A64 York-Malton road, six miles west of Malton

Open daily, except Mondays and Fridays, from Easter Sunday to 1 October

'I have seen gigantic palaces before', wrote Horace Walpole of this mammoth edifice, 'but never a sublime one'. The epithets he used are apt to this day. You approach this very literally great house either by a long drive that begins almost in the village of Coneysthorpe, just west of Malton on a minor road, or by an equally long drive leading off the main road to the south, passing through an imposing gateway and then a glorious double avenue of beech and lime trees. In either case your objective is the hundred-foot-high obelisk designed and built by Vanbrugh, the original architect of the place, in honour of his illustrious patron. It is probably above all the skilful siting of this 'sublime palace' that will make the most immediate impact.

As so often, there has been a building on this commanding site for hundreds of years ;

but Castle Howard is a far more pretentious structure than was the old Henderskelfe Castle that preceded it. It was dramatist-architect Vanbrugh's first essay in design in stone, though he did not in fact live to see the completion of the major project he began in 1700. Work continued throughout much of the eighteenth century, which partly accounts, perhaps, for the impression gained that it grew outwards, so to speak, from a central theme. Huge wings flank the central portion surmounted by the great cupola of Vanbrugh's entrance front of sombre Yorkshire stone.

Within, of course, there is a vast concentration of objects of beauty, either built into the fabric, such as the great Hall Fireplace, the massively pillared chapel and the magnificent vaulting of the Antique Passage ; or the Pre-Raphaelite Group's paintings in the Corridor, the furniture in the Tapestry Room and the Long Gallery, the Holbeins in the Octagon and the Zuccarellis and Carraccis in the Orleans Room.

In the spacious grounds make sure you visit the remarkable Doric Mausoleum and the exquisitely beautiful Temple of the Four Winds ; and, hardly less appealing, the Satyr Gate and the Great Fountain, with its figure of Atlas supporting an enormous globe. Mansion and gardens alike were designed and laid out on the heroic scale.

Yorkshire

Harewood House

On A61 Leeds-Harrogate road, midway between the two towns

Open on Sundays from the end of March to the end of October; also on Tuesdays, Wednesdays and Thursdays from the beginning of May to the end of September

The entrance gates are in Harewood Village, at the crossroads with the main road from Wetherby to Otley, so that this house is less remote, more easily accessible, than many of its contemporaries. Indeed, you become aware of its presence almost before you enter the village, for the village was designed to be all of a piece and is somehow integral with the mansion itself, though existing on its fringe.

Harewood is little more than two centuries old, though the family of the Lascelles who built it had lived in the district for two hundred years before that; it is the Yorkshire seat still, of a descendant of its builder, the Earl of Harewood. As immediately becomes apparent, it was conceived in the palatial mood: first by a Yorkshire architect but almost immediately afterwards by the great Robert Adam himself. The Great Gallery here is generally acknowledged to be among his major masterpieces. The architect, who was to leave his signature so widely scattered about the eighteenth century landscape, worked closely with Chippendale, many of whose finest specimens of craftsmanship are to be seen today in the Old Library, the Princess Royal's Sitting Room, the Green Drawing Room, the dining room, the music room, and in other rooms yet.

As might be expected in a mansion with such a tradition of ownership, rare and priceless works of art, notably pictures, abound. You will see masterpieces by Kaufmann and Reynolds, Hoppner and Lombard, Teniers and Turner, Munnings and Sargent, and a score and more of other artists of similar calibre. You will see silverware and porcelain, tapestry and plasterwork, candelabra and musical instruments and much, much else to

delight the eye and stir the imagination. But it should not be assumed that this house is no more than a museum filled with priceless objects; it is also a home, a connoisseur's home. You will be very conscious of this as you move about from one glorious room to another, and look out through the great windows over the parkland, gardens and ornamental waters of the huge estate. If you are at all knowledgeable about such matters you will almost certainly recognise the hand of 'Capability' Brown in the layout of the grounds from which rises this dignified and splendid mansion, to dominate the setting which lends it added distinction.

Yorkshire

Newby Hall

On B6265, a minor road off A1 just north of Boroughbridge

Open on Wednesdays, Thursdays, Saturdays, Sundays and Bank Holidays from Easter to October

This beautiful house is approached by a mile-long sweeping drive through tree-filled parkland from the end of a winding lane that leaves the Great North Road a few hundred yards north of the bridge spanning the river Ure. Smaller than many of the Yorkshire great houses, it is nevertheless memorable for its red brickwork and stone dressings; it has stood in its ample parkland for two centuries and a half, overlooking the river which flows leisurely past its impressive south front at the foot of the terraced portion of the gardens. It is an extremely interesting example of the successful marrying of two architectural styles and periods: that of Sir Christopher Wren and Robert Adam. It came under Adam's influence because it passed into the hand of a noted collector of sculpture some fifty years after it was built, and he would have no one of lesser calibre than the great architect and designer when it came to the question of housing adequately and elegantly the treasures in statuary that he had so painstakingly acquired in so many of the countries he had been visiting.

So there is indeed within the walls of this edifice a notable display of sculpture, above all in the appropriately named Statue Galleries. Here you should especially look out for the famous Barberini Venus. But it is not by any means all cold statuary that will confront you at Newby Hall. There is Gobelin tapestry; there is a ceiling by Zucchi (Angelica Kaufmann's husband), and another ceiling in the library by Angelica Kaufmann herself. An unusual and most impressive feature, to be found in the entrance hall and on no account to be overlooked, is the beautifully designed and executed Ionic-style organ-case, in rare mahogany, the work of Robert Adam himself, as is so much of the interior of the hall. And there are pictures by Peter Roos, Kneller, Carracci and Raeburn and many other artists, as well as a wealth of fine furniture by various hands and from various periods, notably by Chippendale in his 'French Manner'. All the furniture is skilfully and artistically disposed.

As you leave, glance back within the first hundred yards for a final glimpse of the façade, so serenely beautiful; for the serpentining drive has been so devised as to lead you towards it only when you have come quite close to it.

Alphabetical Index of Houses

Adlington Hall   Cheshire 16
Alnwick Castle   Northumberland 90
Arundel Castle   Sussex 118
Athelhampton   Dorset 38
Audley End House   Essex 44
Avebury Manor   Wiltshire 142

Bateman's   Sussex 120
Beaulieu Abbey   Hampshire 54
Beeleigh Abbey   Essex 46
Belvoir Castle   Leicestershire 74
Berkeley Castle   Gloucestershire 50
Blenheim Palace   Oxfordshire 94
Blickling Hall   Norfolk 80
Blithfield Hall   Staffordshire 106
Breamore House   Hampshire 56
Browsholme Hall   Yorkshire 150
Burghley House   Northamptonshire 84
Burton Agnes Hall   Yorkshire 152

Capesthorne   Cheshire 18
Castle Ashby   Northamptonshire 86
Castle Howard   Yorkshire 154
Chambercombe
  Manor   Devon 34
Charlecote Park   Warwickshire 130
Chartwell Manor   Kent 62
Chatsworth   Derbyshire 26
Clandon Park   Surrey 114
Compton Wynyates   Warwickshire 132
Cothay Manor   Somerset 102
Cothele House   Cornwall 24
Coughton Court   Warwickshire 134
Croft Castle   Herefordshire 58

Dodington House   Gloucestershire 52

Forde Abbey   Dorset 40

Gawsworth Hall   Cheshire 20
Glynde Place   Sussex 122
Great Dixter   Sussex 124
Gunby Hall   Lincolnshire 78

Haddon Hall   Derbyshire 28
Hardwick Hall   Derbyshire 30
Harewood House   Yorkshire 156
Hatfield House   Hertfordshire 60
Hedingham Castle   Essex 48
Hever Castle   Kent 64

Ickworth   Suffolk 110

Levens Hall   Westmorland 140
Little Moreton Hall Cheshire 22
Longleat House   Wiltshire 144

Lydiard Mansion   Wiltshire 146

Melbourne Hall   Derbyshire 32
Melford Hall   Suffolk 112
Mereworth Castle   Kent 66
Montacute House   Somerset 104

Newby Hall   Yorkshire 158
Newstead Abbey   Nottinghamshire 92

Oxburgh Hall   Norfolk 82

Packwood House   Warwickshire 136
Parham   Sussex 126
Penshurst Place   Kent 68
Petworth House   Sussex 128
Polesden Lacey   Surrey 116
Powderham Castle   Devon 36

Raby Castle   Co. Durham 42
Ragley Hall   Warwickshire 138
Rousham House   Oxfordshire 96
Rufford Old Hall   Lancashire 72

Sawston Hall   Cambridgeshire 14
Stapleford Park   Leicestershire 76
Stokesay Castle   Shropshire 98
Sulgrave Manor   Northamptonshire 88

Walmer Castle   Kent 70
West Wycombe Park   Buckinghamshire 12
Weston Park   Shropshire 100
Wightwick Manor   Staffordshire 108
Wilton House   Wiltshire 148
Woburn Abbey   Bedfordshire 10

Scotland

1

Northumb.

Cumberland

Co. Durham

Westmd.

3

2

9

7

Yorkshire

5

8

6

Lancashire

4

Cheshire

10

12

11

13

18

19

20

Notts.

Lincolnshire

23

Derby.

21

22

Staffs.

16

30

31

Rutd.

36

37

Norfolk

Leics.

32

15

17

Shrops.

Wales

14

Worcs.

28

27

29

Warwicks.

25

Northants.

33

Hunts.

35

44

Suffolk

45

Cambs.

24

Herefs.

26

34

Beds.

43

47

49

41

Oxon.

Bucks.

Herts.

Essex

Glos.

40

46

48

Mon.

38

42

Middx.

London

39

59

Berks.

71

73

57

Surrey

Kent

51

Wiltshire

58

63

64

72

74

75

Somerset

53

60

Hampshire

70

69

Sussex

66

68

54

62

65

67

55

Devon

Dorset

61

52

56

50

Cornwall